Germany 1918 - 1945

GCSE HISTORY REVISION IN SPIDER DIAGRAMS

A H Goddard

Copyright © 2018 by Alistair Goddard

First Published in 2018

All rights reserved. No part of this publication may be reproduced, distributed, or transmitted in any form or by any means, including photocopying, recording, or other electronic or mechanical methods, without the prior written permission of the publisher, except in accordance with the provisions of the Copyright, Designs and Patents Act 1988 or under the terms of a licence issued by the Copyright Licensing Agency.

ISBN-13: 978-1978329843
ISBN-10: 1978329849

Contents

Was the Weimar Republic doomed to failure?

What happened during the November Revolution (1918)?	2
What problems did Germany face at the end of the First World War?	3
What happened during the Spartacist Uprising (1919)?	4
What happened during the Kapp Putsch (1920)?	4
What were the strengths and weaknesses of the Weimar Constitution?	5
What were the terms of the Versailles Treaty?	6
What was the economic and political impact of the Versailles Treaty (1919)?	6
What crises did the Weimar Republic face in 1923?	7
How did Chancellor Stresemann deal with the crises of 1923?	8
How did the Nazi Party develop before 1923?	9
What did Hitler and the Nazis stand for in the 1920s?	10
What happened during the Munich Putsch (1923)?	11
How did Hitler benefit from the Munich Putsch (1923)?	11
Why did Hitler think the Munich Putsch would work?	11
How far did the Weimar Republic recover in the period 1924-29?	12

Why was Hitler able to become Führer by 1934?

How did the Nazis change their tactics in the period 1924-29?	13
Why were the Nazis not successful in the period 1924-29?	13
What were the roles of Nazi leaders?	14
What impact did the Great Depression have on the Weimar Republic?	15
How did Hitler become Chancellor in 1933?	15
What was the Reichstag Fire (1933)?	16
How did the Reichstag Fire benefit Hitler?	16
Why did Hitler become Chancellor in 1933? (Part 1)	17
Why did Hitler become Chancellor in 1933? (Part 2)	18
What was the Enabling Act (March 1933)?	19
How did the Enabling Act benefit Hitler?	19

Why were Röhm and the SA seen as a threat by Hitler? 20
How did Hitler become President in 1934? 19
Why did Hitler make the army swear an oath to him in 1934? 19
What happened during the Night of the Long Knives (1934)? 20
Was the Weimar Republic a success or a failure? 21

How effective were Nazi efforts to control Germany, 1933-45?

How did the Nazis use propaganda? 22
How successful was Nazi propaganda? 23
What was the role of the SS and Gestapo? What were concentration camps? 24
How effective was the Gestapo at controlling the German population? 25
How did the Nazis control education? 26
Why did children join the Hitler Youth and the League of German Maidens? 26
Why did the Nazis want to influence young people? 26
How successful were Nazi policies towards young people? 27
What were Nazi policies towards women? 28
How successful were Nazi policies towards women? 28
What was wrong with the German economy in 1933? 29
How did the Nazis reduce unemployment? 29
How successful were Nazi economic policies?
Did Nazi economic policies make people's lives better? 30
How much opposition was there to the Nazis? 31
Why did the Nazis persecute certain groups? 32
What was the impact of the Second World War (1939-45) on ordinary life in Germany? 33
How did the Nazis persecute Jews? 34
What happened on Kristallnacht (1938)? 34
Why was there little opposition to the Nazis?
How did the Nazis control the German people? 35
Were German people better off under the Nazis? 36

Revision Tracking List 37

Time line

1918	Armistice ends First World War
1918	November Revolution
1919	Spartacist Uprising
1919	Versailles Treaty
1919	Hitler joins German Workers' Party
1920	Kapp Putsch
1920	Nazis publish 25 Points
1920	Hitler becomes Nazi leader
1923	Occupation of the Ruhr
1923	Hyperinflation
1923	Munich Putsch
1925	Locarno Treaties
1926	Germany joins League of Nations
1928	German industrial production reaches pre-war levels
1928	Nazis gain 12 seats in Reichstag elections
1929	Beginning of Great Depression
1930	Nazis gain 107 seats in Reichstag elections
1932	Nazis gain 230 seats in Reichstag elections
1933	Hitler appointed as Chancellor
1933	Reichstag Fire
1933	Nazis gain 288 seats in Reichstag elections
1934	Enabling Act
1934	Night of the Long Knives
1934	Hitler becomes President
1935	Nuremberg Laws
1935	Conscription reintroduced
1937	Change in policy towards women
1938	Kristallknacht
1939	Second World War begins
1942	The "Final Solution" begins
1944	Army bomb plot to assassinate Hitler
1945	End of Second World War

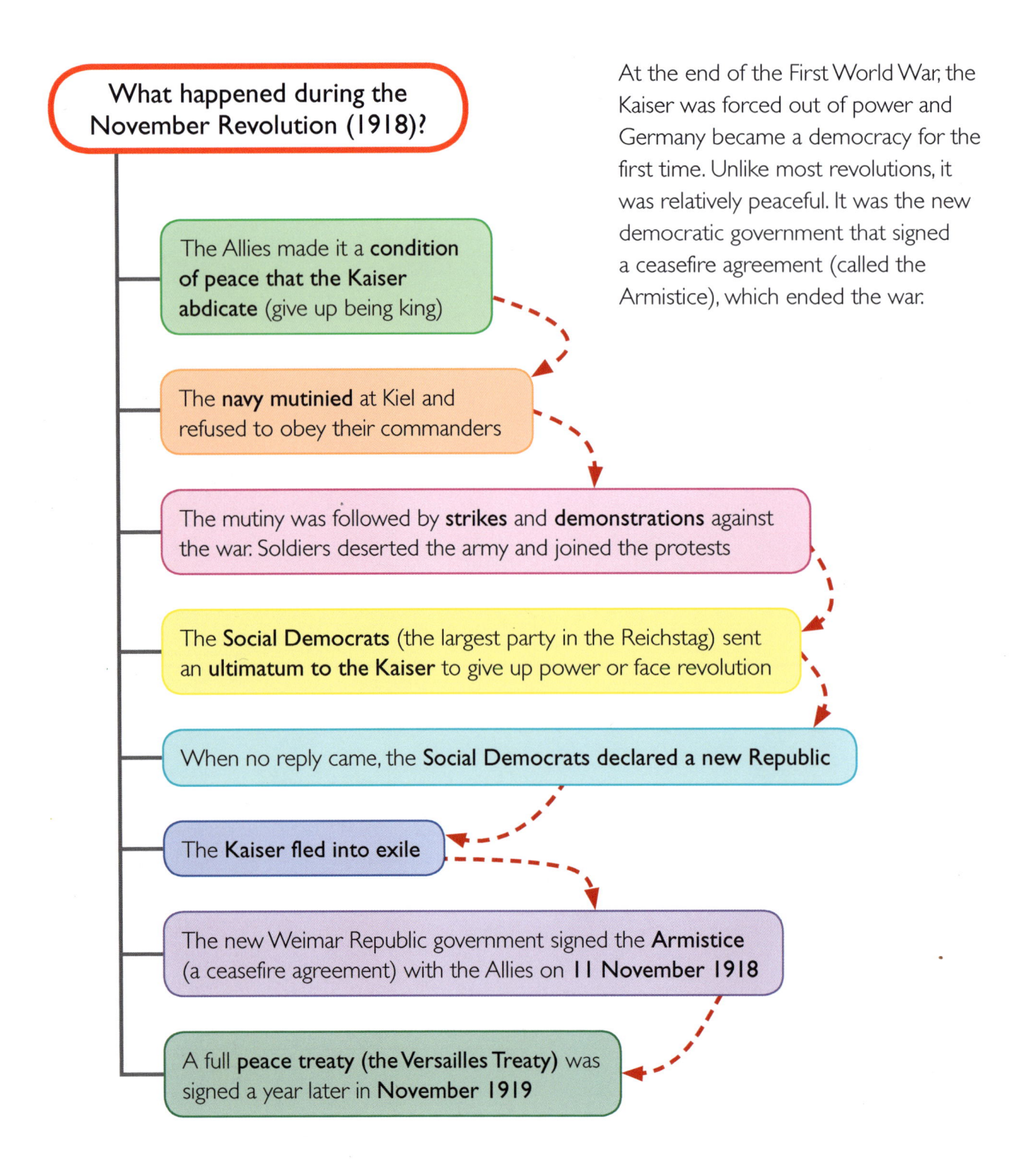

What happened during the November Revolution (1918)?

At the end of the First World War, the Kaiser was forced out of power and Germany became a democracy for the first time. Unlike most revolutions, it was relatively peaceful. It was the new democratic government that signed a ceasefire agreement (called the Armistice), which ended the war.

- The Allies made it a **condition of peace that the Kaiser abdicate** (give up being king)

- The **navy mutinied** at Kiel and refused to obey their commanders

- The mutiny was followed by **strikes** and **demonstrations** against the war. Soldiers deserted the army and joined the protests

- The **Social Democrats** (the largest party in the Reichstag) sent an **ultimatum to the Kaiser** to give up power or face revolution

- When no reply came, the **Social Democrats declared a new Republic**

- The **Kaiser fled into exile**

- The new Weimar Republic government signed the **Armistice** (a ceasefire agreement) with the Allies on **11 November 1918**

- A full **peace treaty (the Versailles Treaty)** was signed a year later in **November 1919**

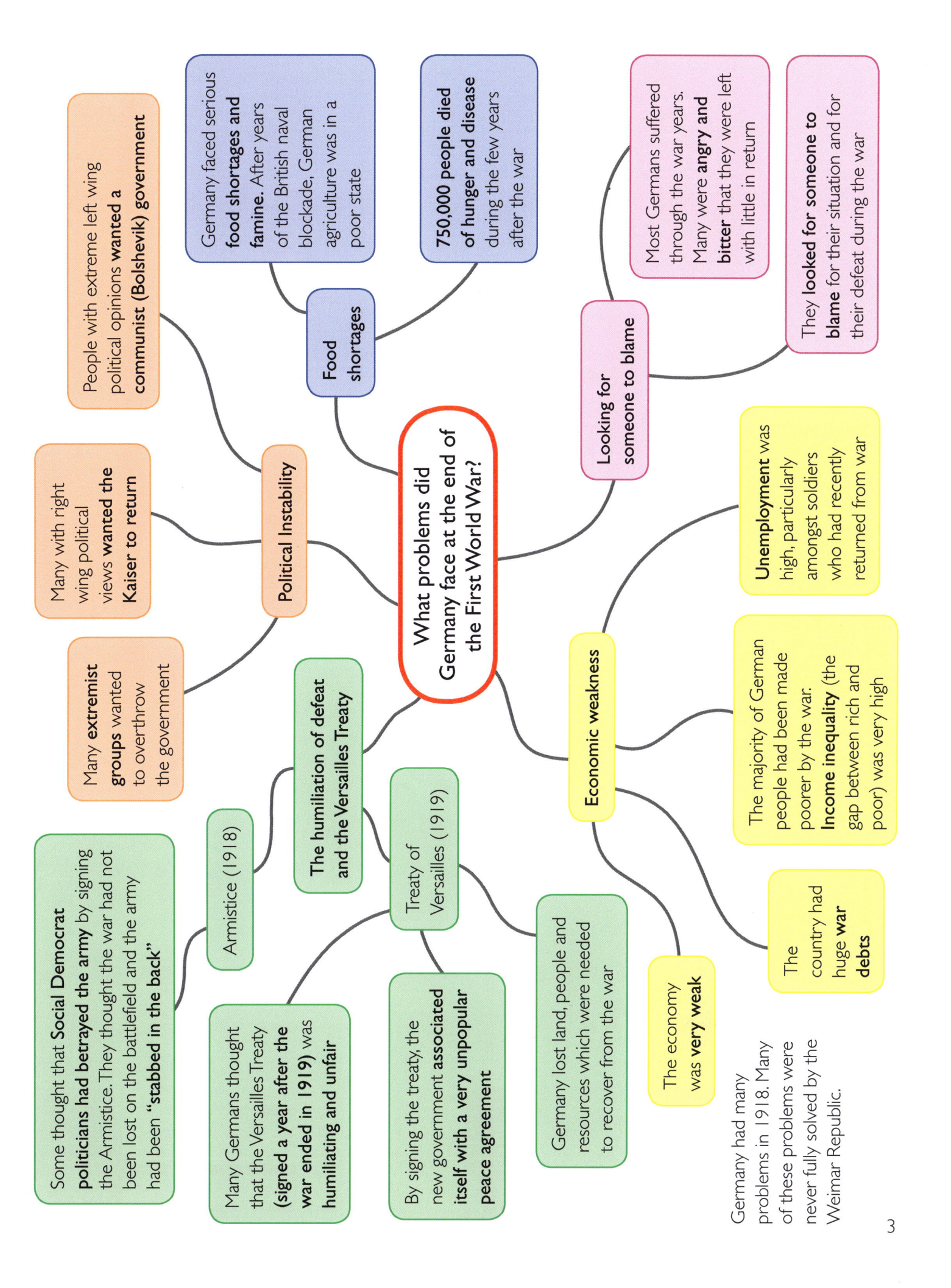

What problems did Germany face at the end of the First World War?

Political Instability

- People with extreme left wing political opinions **wanted a communist (Bolshevik) government**
- Many with right wing political views **wanted the Kaiser to return**
- Many **extremist groups** wanted to overthrow the government

Food shortages

- Germany faced serious **food shortages and famine**. After years of the British naval blockade, German agriculture was in a poor state
- **750,000 people died of hunger and disease** during the few years after the war

Looking for someone to blame

- Most Germans suffered through the war years. Many were **angry and bitter** that they were left with little in return
- They **looked for someone to blame** for their situation and for their defeat during the war

The humiliation of defeat and the Versailles Treaty

- Armistice (1918)
- Treaty of Versailles (1919)
- Some thought that Social Democrat **politicians had betrayed the army** by signing the Armistice. They thought the war had not been lost on the battlefield and the army had been **"stabbed in the back"**
- Many Germans thought that the Versailles Treaty **(signed a year after the war ended in 1919)** was humiliating and unfair
- By signing the treaty, the new government **associated itself with a very unpopular peace agreement**
- Germany lost land, people and resources which were needed to recover from the war

Economic weakness

- Unemployment was high, particularly amongst soldiers who had recently returned from war
- The majority of German people had been made poorer by the war. **Income inequality** (the gap between rich and poor) was very high
- The country had huge **war debts**
- The economy was **very weak**

Germany had many problems in 1918. Many of these problems were never fully solved by the Weimar Republic.

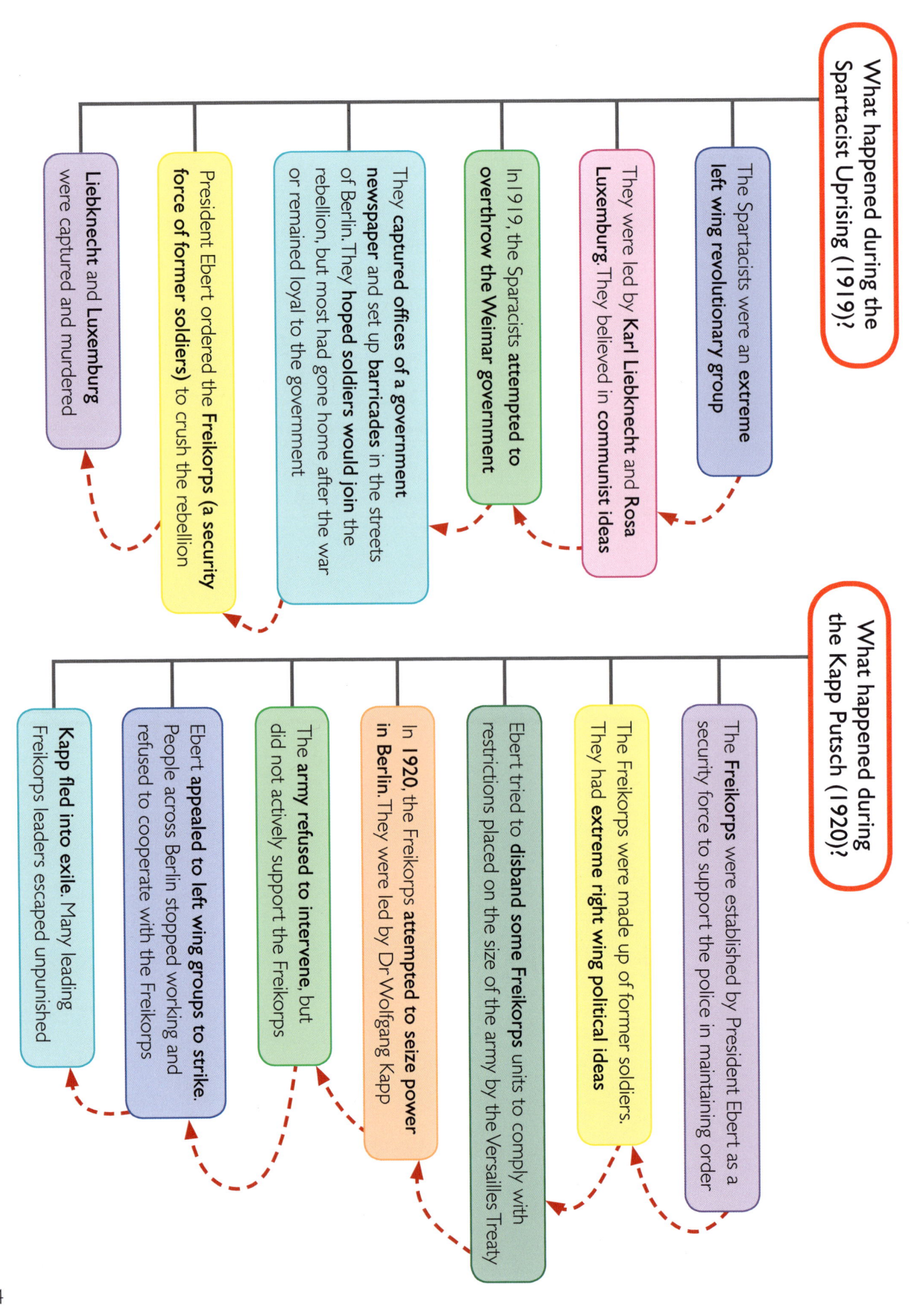

What happened during the Spartacist Uprising (1919)?

- The Spartacists were an extreme **left wing revolutionary group**
- They were led by **Karl Liebknecht** and **Rosa Luxemburg**. They believed in **communist ideas**
- In 1919, the Spartacists attempted to **overthrow the Weimar government**
- They captured offices of a government newspaper and set up **barricades** in the streets of Berlin. They **hoped soldiers would join the rebellion**, but most had gone home after the war or remained loyal to the government
- President Ebert ordered the **Freikorps (a security force of former soldiers)** to crush the rebellion
- **Liebknecht and Luxemburg** were captured and murdered

What happened during the Kapp Putsch (1920)?

- The **Freikorps** were established by President Ebert as a security force to support the police in maintaining order
- The Freikorps were made up of former soldiers. They had **extreme right wing political ideas**
- Ebert tried to **disband some Freikorps** units to comply with restrictions placed on the size of the army by the Versailles Treaty
- In **1920**, the Freikorps **attempted to seize power in Berlin**. They were led by Dr Wolfgang Kapp
- The **army refused to intervene**, but did not actively support the Freikorps
- Ebert **appealed to left wing groups to strike**. People across Berlin stopped working and refused to cooperate with the Freikorps
- **Kapp fled into exile**. Many leading Freikorps leaders escaped unpunished

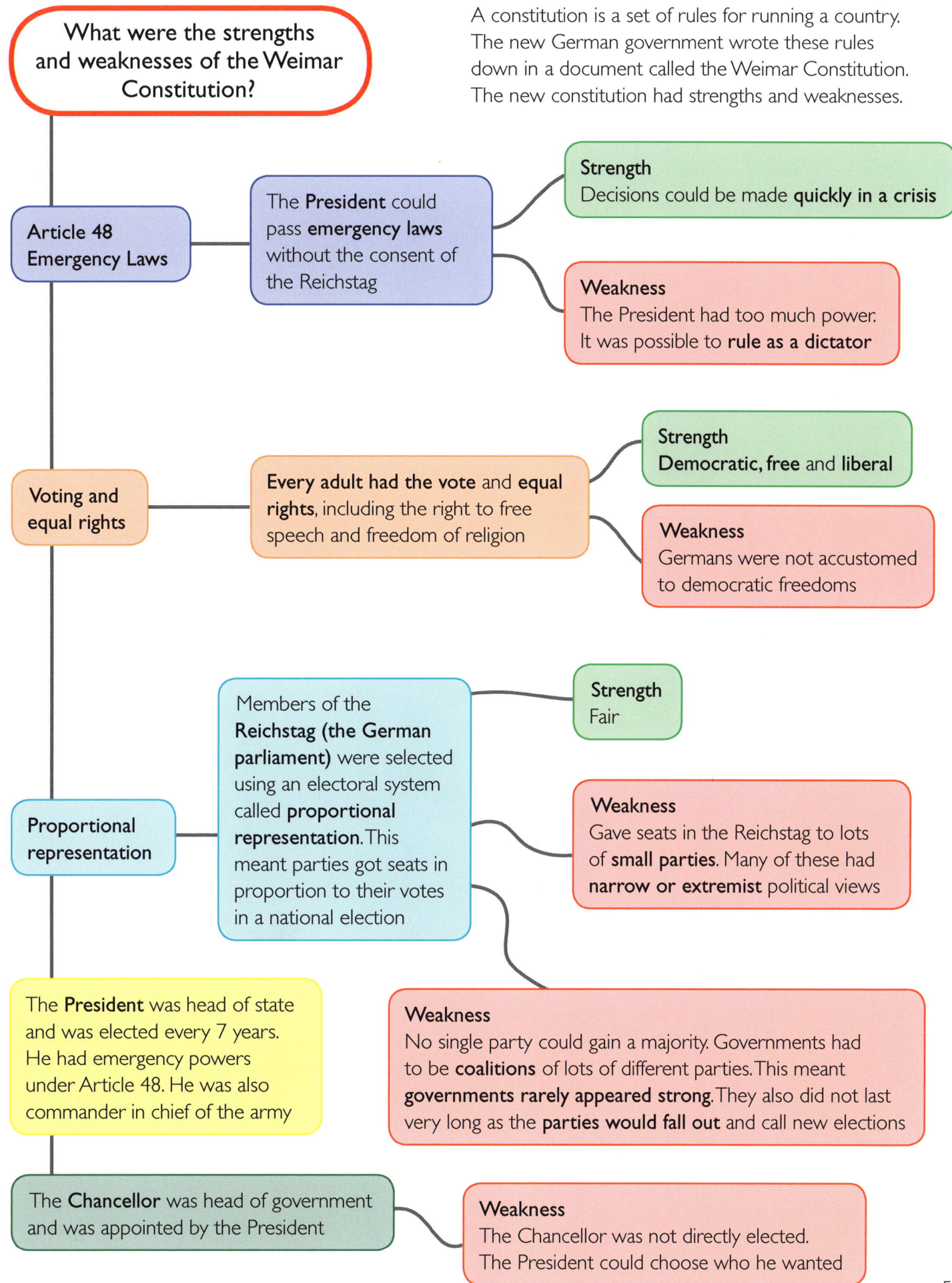

What were the strengths and weaknesses of the Weimar Constitution?

A constitution is a set of rules for running a country. The new German government wrote these rules down in a document called the Weimar Constitution. The new constitution had strengths and weaknesses.

Article 48 Emergency Laws — The **President** could pass **emergency laws** without the consent of the Reichstag

- **Strength**: Decisions could be made **quickly in a crisis**
- **Weakness**: The President had too much power. It was possible to **rule as a dictator**

Voting and equal rights — **Every adult had the vote** and **equal rights**, including the right to free speech and freedom of religion

- **Strength**: Democratic, free and liberal
- **Weakness**: Germans were not accustomed to democratic freedoms

Proportional representation — Members of the **Reichstag (the German parliament)** were selected using an electoral system called **proportional representation**. This meant parties got seats in proportion to their votes in a national election

- **Strength**: Fair
- **Weakness**: Gave seats in the Reichstag to lots of **small parties**. Many of these had **narrow or extremist** political views
- **Weakness**: No single party could gain a majority. Governments had to be **coalitions** of lots of different parties. This meant **governments rarely appeared strong**. They also did not last very long as the **parties would fall out** and call new elections

The **President** was head of state and was elected every 7 years. He had emergency powers under Article 48. He was also commander in chief of the army

The **Chancellor** was head of government and was appointed by the President

- **Weakness**: The Chancellor was not directly elected. The President could choose who he wanted

What were the terms of the Versailles Treaty?

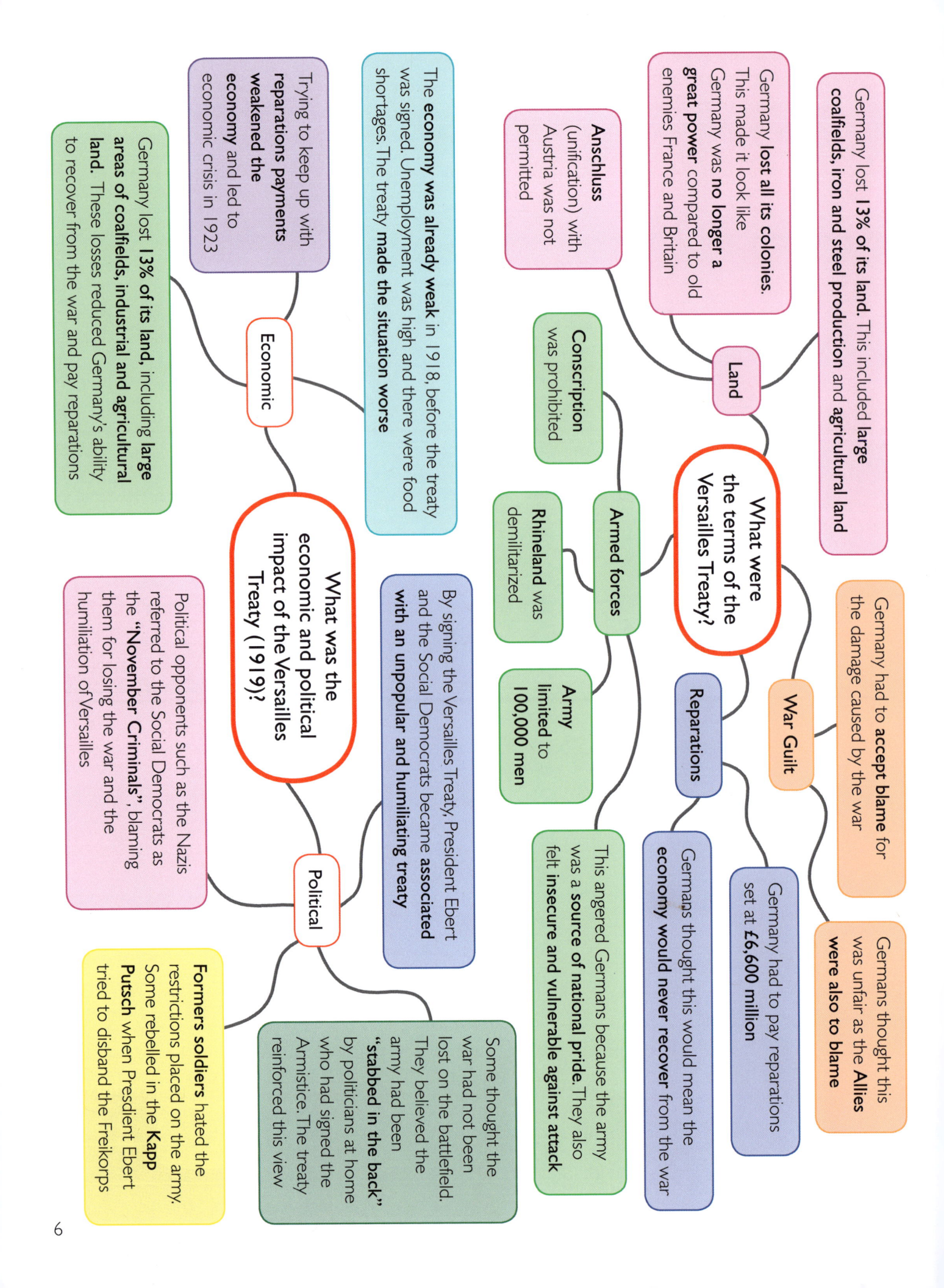

Land

- Germany lost 13% of its land. This included large coalfields, iron and steel production and agricultural land
- Germany lost all its colonies. This made it look like Germany was **no longer a great power** compared to old enemies France and Britain
- **Anschluss** (unification) with Austria was not permitted

Armed forces

- Conscription was prohibited
- **Rhineland** was demilitarized
- Army limited to 100,000 men

War Guilt

- Germany had to **accept blame** for the damage caused by the war
- Germans thought this was unfair as the **Allies were also to blame**

Reparations

- Germany had to pay reparations set at £6,600 million
- Germans thought this would mean the **economy would never recover from the war**
- This angered Germans because the army was a **source of national pride**. They also felt **insecure and vulnerable against attack**

What was the economic and political impact of the Versailles Treaty (1919)?

Economic

- Germany lost 13% of its land, including **large areas of coalfields, industrial and agricultural land**. These losses reduced Germany's ability to recover from the war and pay reparations
- Trying to keep up with **reparations payments weakened the economy** and led to economic crisis in 1923
- The **economy was already weak** in 1918, before the treaty was signed. Unemployment was high and there were food shortages. The treaty **made the situation worse**

Political

- By signing the Versailles Treaty, President Ebert and the Social Democrats became **associated with an unpopular and humiliating treaty**
- Political opponents such as the Nazis referred to the Social Democrats as the **"November Criminals"**, blaming them for losing the war and the humiliation of Versailles
- Some thought the war had not been lost on the battlefield. They believed the army had been **"stabbed in the back"** by politicians at home who had signed the Armistice. The treaty reinforced this view
- Former **soldiers hated** the restrictions placed on the army. Some rebelled in the **Kapp Putsch** when President Ebert tried to disband the Freikorps

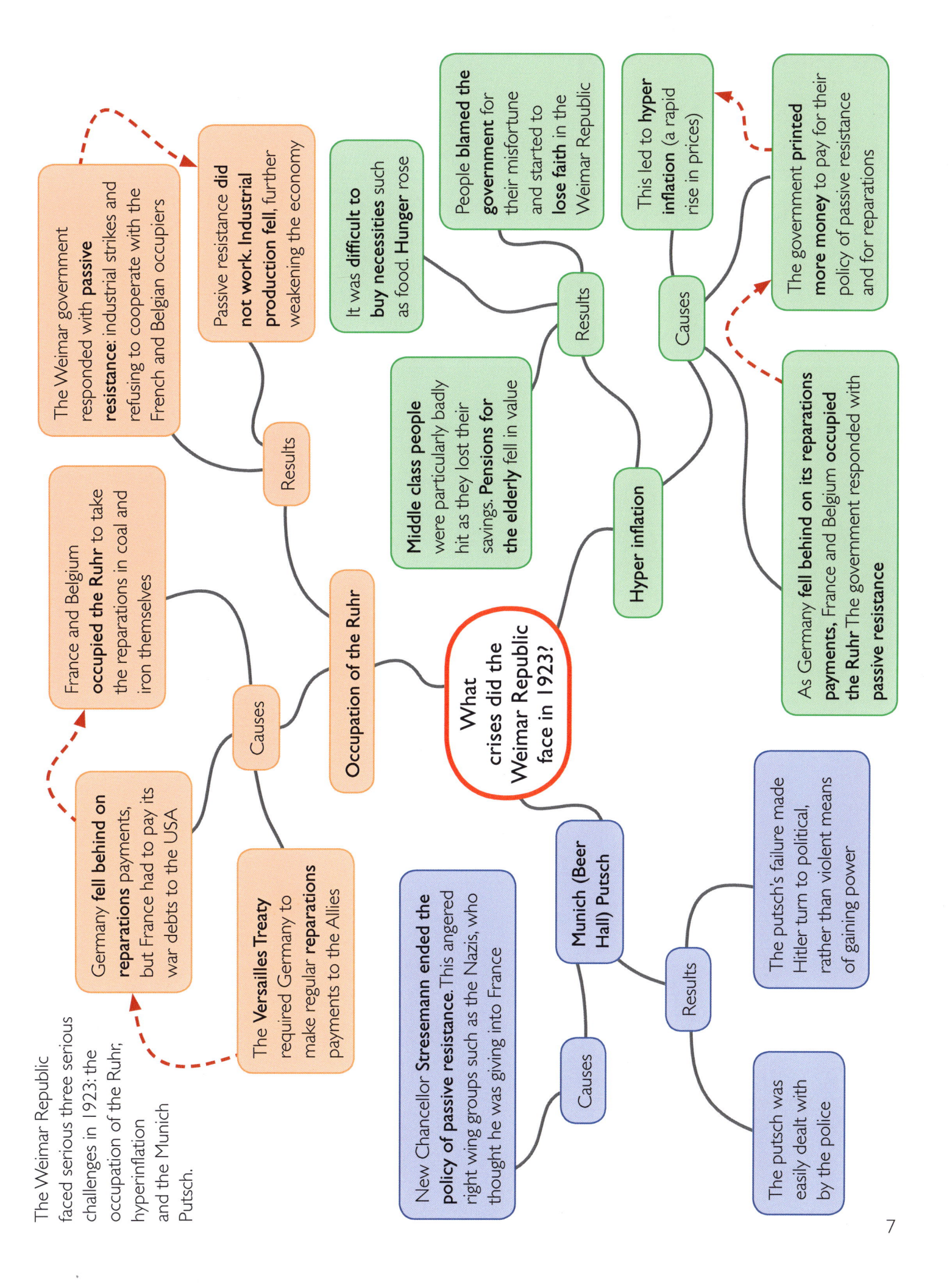

The Weimar Republic faced serious three serious challenges in 1923: the occupation of the Ruhr, hyperinflation and the Munich Putsch.

What crises did the Weimar Republic face in 1923?

Occupation of the Ruhr

Causes:
- The **Versailles Treaty** required Germany to make regular **reparations** payments to the Allies
- Germany **fell behind** on **reparations** payments, but France had to pay its war debts to the USA
- France and Belgium **occupied the Ruhr** to take the reparations in coal and iron themselves

Results:
- The Weimar government responded with **passive resistance**: industrial strikes and refusing to cooperate with the French and Belgian occupiers
- Passive resistance **did not work. Industrial production fell**, further weakening the economy

Hyper inflation

Causes:
- As Germany **fell behind on its reparations payments**, France and Belgium **occupied the Ruhr** The government responded with **passive resistance**
- The government **printed more money** to pay for their policy of passive resistance and for reparations
- This led to **hyper inflation** (a rapid rise in prices)

Results:
- It was **difficult to buy necessities** such as food. **Hunger** rose
- **Middle class people** were particularly badly hit as they lost their savings. **Pensions for the elderly** fell in value
- People **blamed the government** for their misfortune and started to **lose faith** in the Weimar Republic

Munich (Beer Hall) Putsch

Causes:
- New Chancellor **Stresemann ended the policy of passive resistance.** This angered right wing groups such as the Nazis, who thought he was giving into France

Results:
- The putsch was easily dealt with by the police
- The putsch's failure made Hitler turn to political, rather than violent means of gaining power

7

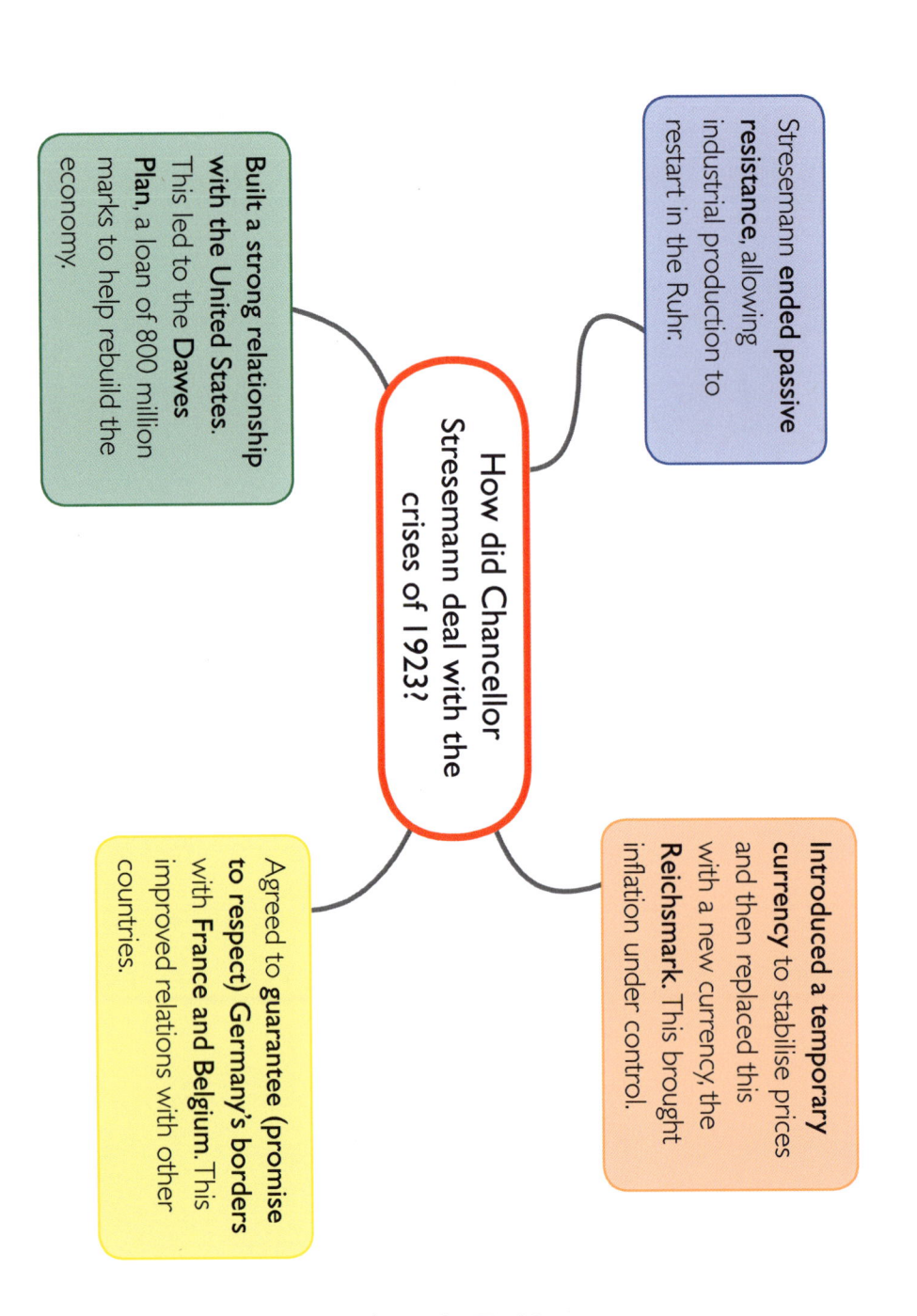

How did Chancellor Stresemann deal with the crises of 1923?

- **Stresemann ended passive resistance**, allowing industrial production to restart in the Ruhr.

- **Built a strong relationship with the United States.** This led to the **Dawes Plan**, a loan of 800 million marks to help rebuild the economy.

- **Introduced a temporary currency** to stabilise prices and then replaced this with a new currency, the **Reichsmark**. This brought inflation under control.

- **Agreed to guarantee (promise to respect) Germany's borders** with **France and Belgium**. This improved relations with other countries.

Stresemann served for a short period as Chancellor and then as foreign minister. The period 1923–1929 is sometimes called the Stresemann Era.

What did the SA do for the Nazis?

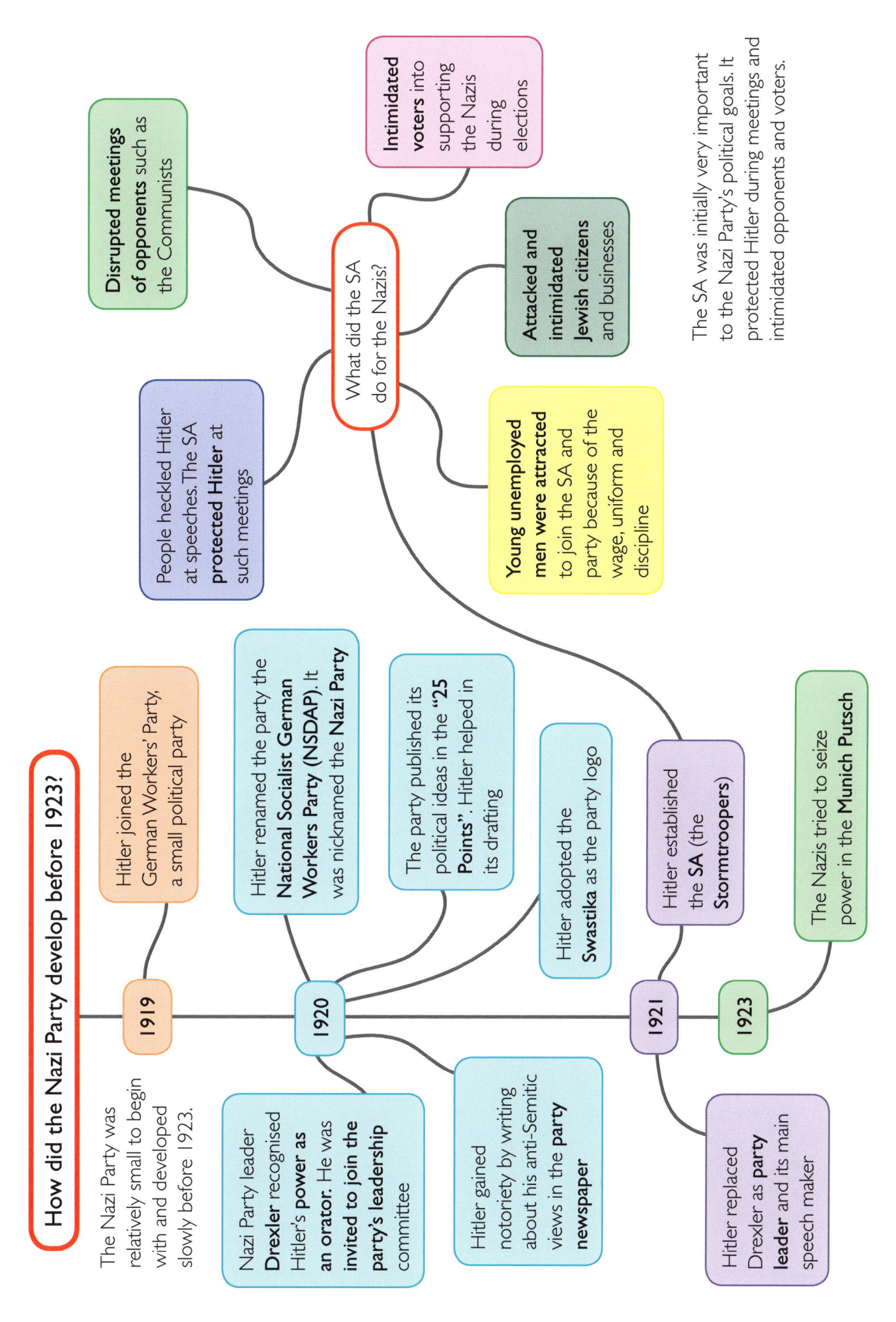

- **Disrupted meetings of opponents** such as the Communists
- **Intimidated voters** into supporting the Nazis during elections
- **Attacked and intimidated Jewish citizens** and businesses
- People heckled Hitler at speeches. The SA **protected Hitler** at such meetings
- **Young unemployed men were attracted** to join the SA and party because of the wage, uniform and discipline

The SA was initially very important to the Nazi Party's political goals. It protected Hitler during meetings and intimidated opponents and voters.

How did the Nazi Party develop before 1923?

The Nazi Party was relatively small to begin with and developed slowly before 1923.

1919
- Hitler joined the German Workers' Party, a small political party

1920
- Nazi Party leader **Drexler** recognised Hitler's power as an orator. He was **invited to join the party's leadership** committee
- Hitler renamed the party the **National Socialist German Workers Party (NSDAP)**. It was nicknamed the Nazi Party
- The party published its political ideas in the **"25 Points"**. Hitler helped in its drafting
- Hitler adopted the **Swastika** as the party logo
- Hitler gained notoriety by writing about his anti-Semitic views in the **party newspaper**

1921
- Hitler established the **SA (the Stormtroopers)**
- Hitler replaced Drexler as **party leader** and its main speech maker

1923
- The Nazis tried to seize power in the **Munich Putsch**

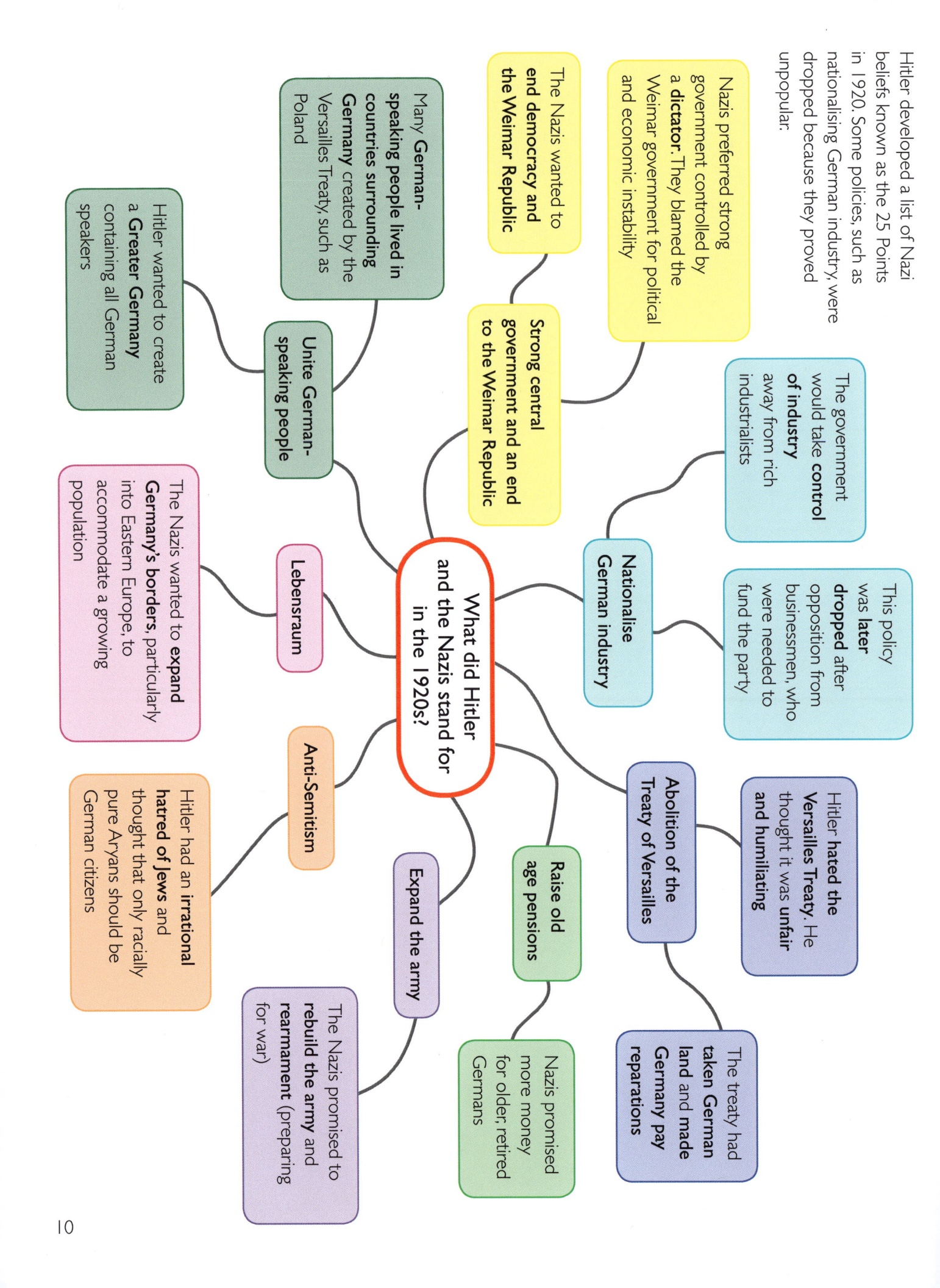

Hitler developed a list of Nazi beliefs known as the 25 Points in 1920. Some policies, such as nationalising German industry, were dropped because they proved unpopular.

What did Hitler and the Nazis stand for in the 1920s?

Strong central government and an end to the Weimar Republic
- The Nazis wanted to **end democracy and the Weimar Republic**
- Nazis preferred strong government controlled by a **dictator**. They blamed the Weimar government for political and economic instability

Nationalise German industry
- The government would take **control of industry** away from rich industrialists
- This policy was **later dropped** after opposition from businessmen, who were needed to fund the party

Unite German-speaking people
- Many German-speaking people lived in countries surrounding **Germany** created by the Versailles Treaty, such as Poland
- Hitler wanted to create a **Greater Germany** containing all German speakers

Lebensraum
- The Nazis wanted to **expand Germany's borders**, particularly into Eastern Europe, to accommodate a growing population

Anti-Semitism
- Hitler had an **irrational hatred of Jews** and thought that only racially pure Aryans should be German citizens

Expand the army
- The Nazis promised to **rebuild the army and rearmament** (preparing for war)

Raise old age pensions
- Nazis promised more money for older, retired Germans

Abolition of the Treaty of Versailles
- Hitler **hated the Versailles Treaty**. He thought it was **unfair and humiliating**
- The treaty had **taken German land and made Germany pay reparations**

What happened during the Munich Putsch (1923):

- Stresemann ended the policy of passive resistance in the Ruhr. This angered many right wing supporters
- Hitler believed it was time to seize power. Hitler was supported by Ludendorff, a senior army general
- The Nazis interrupted a political meeting held in a Munich beer hall addressed by the right wing Bavarian chancellor Kahr. Hitler tried to persuade Kahr to support a rebellion attempt
- The following day, the Nazis tried to take control of Munich. Kahr failed to support Hitler and the putsch was crushed by the police and army, which remained loyal to the Republic
- Hitler and Ludendorff were arrested and placed on trial. Hitler's speeches in court persuaded the judges to give lenient sentences

How did Hitler benefit from the Munich Putsch (1923)? (3 Ps)

Publicity
- Before 1923, Nazi support was concentrated around Munich and in South Germany
- Hitler spread his political views by speaking at his trial. His opinions were reported internationally in newspaper coverage
- The trial gave Hitler a national reputation as a passionate and persuasive political leader

Penning Mein Kampf
- His time in prison gave Hitler an opportunity to write Mein Kampf, a bestselling account of his life and explanation of his political views. It was used as a manifesto in future elections

Power through politics
- Hitler realised he needed to change his political strategy: gaining power using the political system rather than through an armed rebellion

Why did Hitler think the Munich Putsch would work?

Important people supportive
- Von Kahr, the leader of the Bavarian regional government, was right wing and wanted to overthrow the government
- Former army leader General Ludendorff supported the Nazis. He suggested that he could convince the army to support the rebellion

Public anger
- Many had suffered because of hyperinflation and blamed the government
- Stresemann's decision to end passive resistance was very unpopular. It looked like he was giving into France

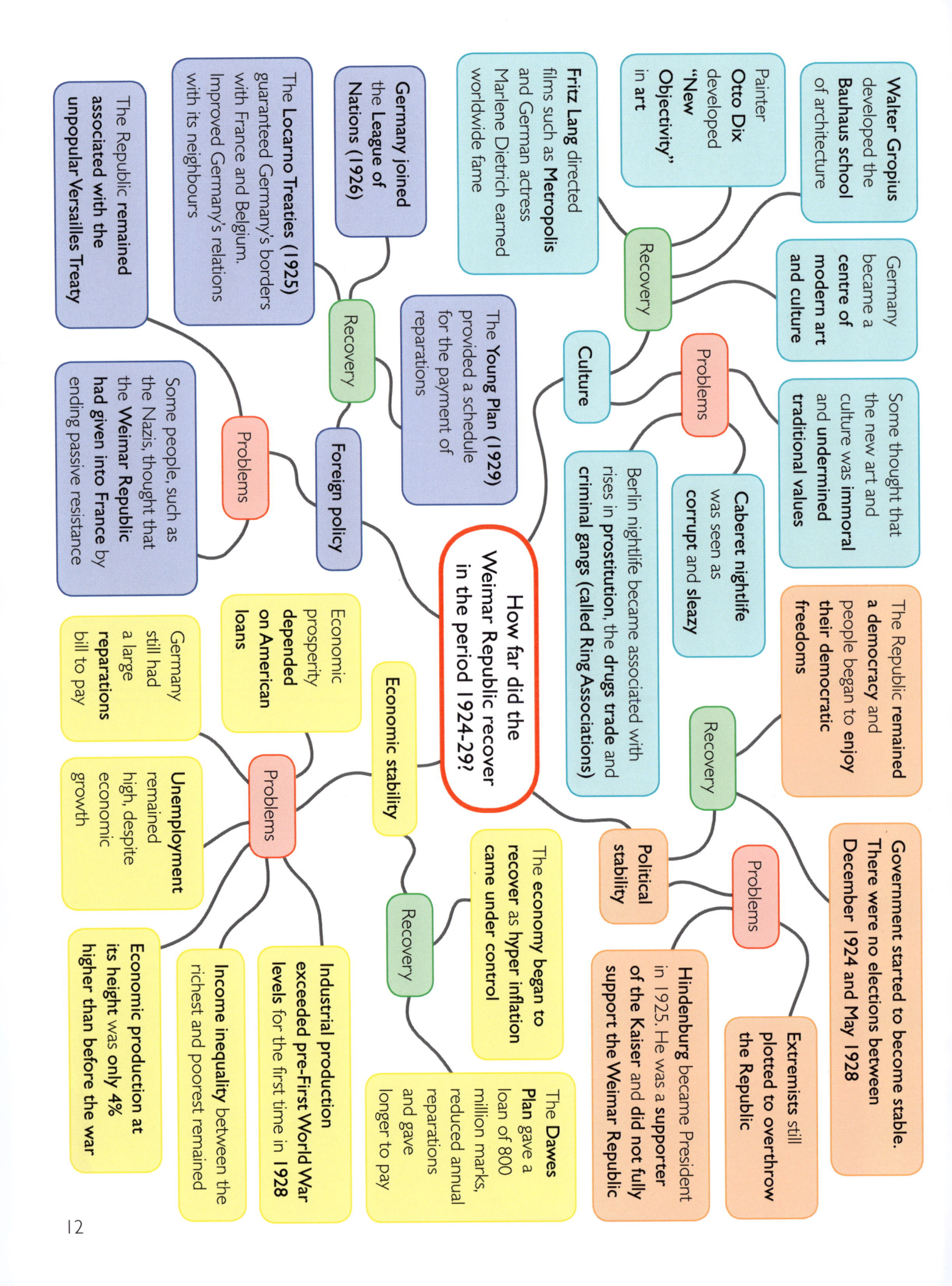

How far did the Weimar Republic recover in the period 1924-29?

Culture

Recovery
- Walter Gropius developed the **Bauhaus school** of architecture
- Painter **Otto Dix** developed **"New Objectivity"** in art
- Fritz Lang directed films such as **Metropolis** and German actress Marlene Dietrich earned worldwide fame
- Germany became a centre of **modern art and culture**

Problems
- Some thought that the new art and culture was **immoral** and undermined **traditional values**
- Caberet nightlife was seen as **corrupt** and **sleazy**
- Berlin nightlife became associated with rises in **prostitution**, the **drugs trade** and **criminal gangs** (called Ring Associations)

Foreign policy

Recovery
- Germany joined the **League of Nations (1926)**
- The **Locarno Treaties (1925)** guaranteed Germany's borders with France and Belgium. Improved Germany's relations with its neighbours
- The **Young Plan (1929)** provided a schedule for the payment of reparations

Problems
- The Republic remained **associated with the unpopular Versailles Treaty**
- Some people, such as the Nazis, thought that the **Weimar Republic had given into France** by ending passive resistance

Economic stability

Recovery
- The economy began to recover as hyper inflation came under control
- The **Dawes Plan** gave a loan of 800 million marks, reduced annual reparations and gave longer to pay
- Industrial production exceeded pre-First World War levels for the first time in **1928**

Problems
- Economic prosperity depended on **American loans**
- Germany still had a large **reparations** bill to pay
- **Unemployment** remained high, despite economic growth
- Income inequality between the richest and poorest remained
- Economic production at its height was only 4% higher than before the war

Political stability

Recovery
- The Republic remained **a democracy** and people began to enjoy **their democratic freedoms**
- Hindenburg became President in 1925. He was **a supporter of the Kaiser and did not fully support the Weimar Republic**

Problems
- Government started to become stable. There were no elections between December 1924 and May 1928
- Extremists still **plotted to overthrow the Republic**

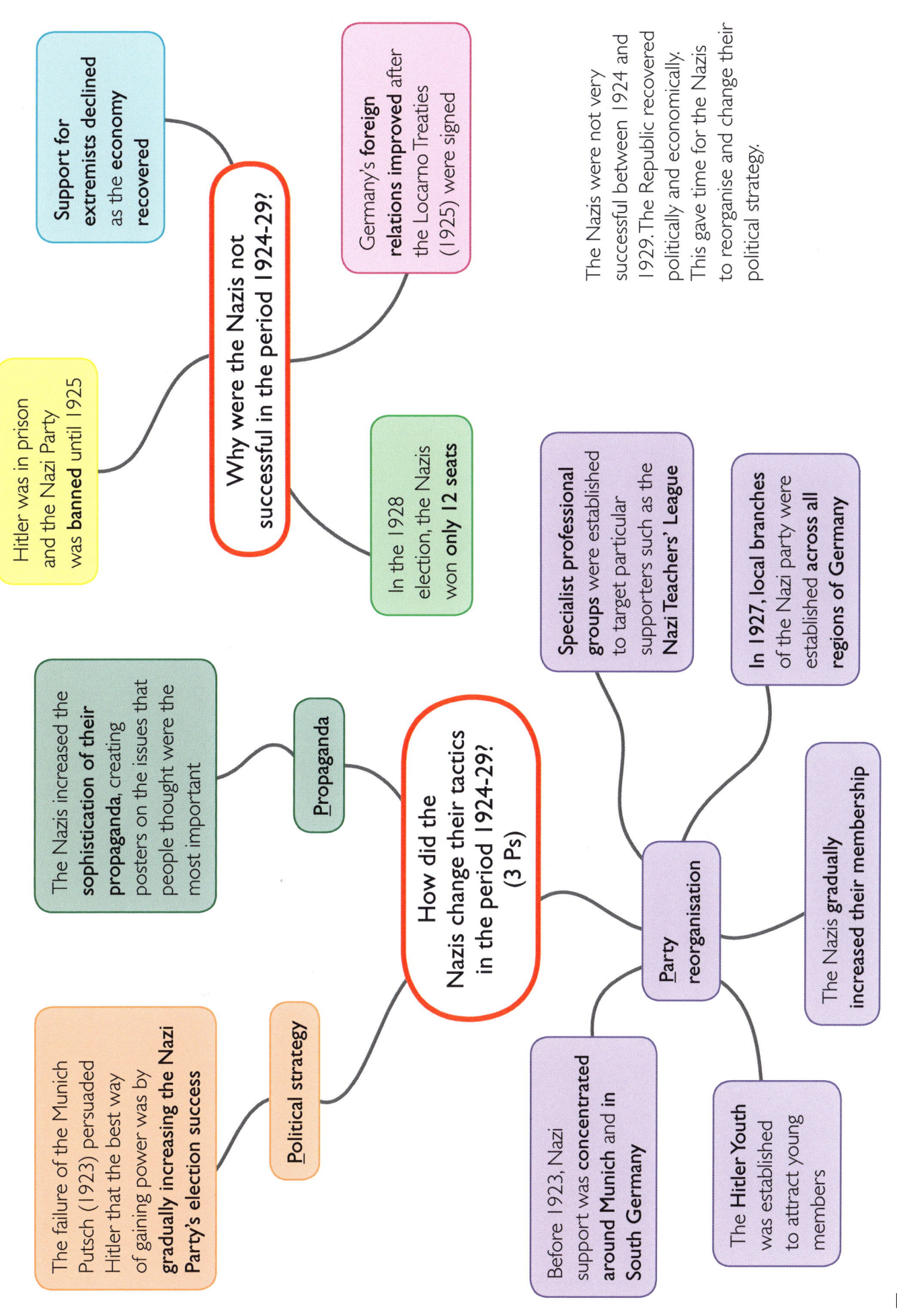

Why were the Nazis not successful in the period 1924-29?

- **Support for extremists declined** as the economy recovered
- Germany's **foreign relations improved** after the Locarno Treaties (1925) were signed
- Hitler was in prison and the Nazi Party was **banned** until 1925
- In the 1928 election, the Nazis won **only 12 seats**

The Nazis were not very successful between 1924 and 1929. The Republic recovered politically and economically. This gave time for the Nazis to reorganise and change their political strategy.

How did the Nazis change their tactics in the period 1924-29? (3 Ps)

Propaganda
- The Nazis increased the **sophistication of their propaganda**, creating posters on the issues that people thought were the most important

Political strategy
- The failure of the Munich Putsch (1923) persuaded Hitler that the best way of gaining power was by **gradually increasing the Nazi Party's election success**

Party reorganisation
- **Specialist professional groups** were established to target particular supporters such as the **Nazi Teachers' League**
- In **1927, local branches** of the Nazi party were established **across all regions of Germany**
- The Nazis gradually increased their membership
- Before 1923, Nazi support was **concentrated around Munich and in South Germany**
- The **Hitler Youth** was established to attract young members

13

What were the roles of Nazi leaders?

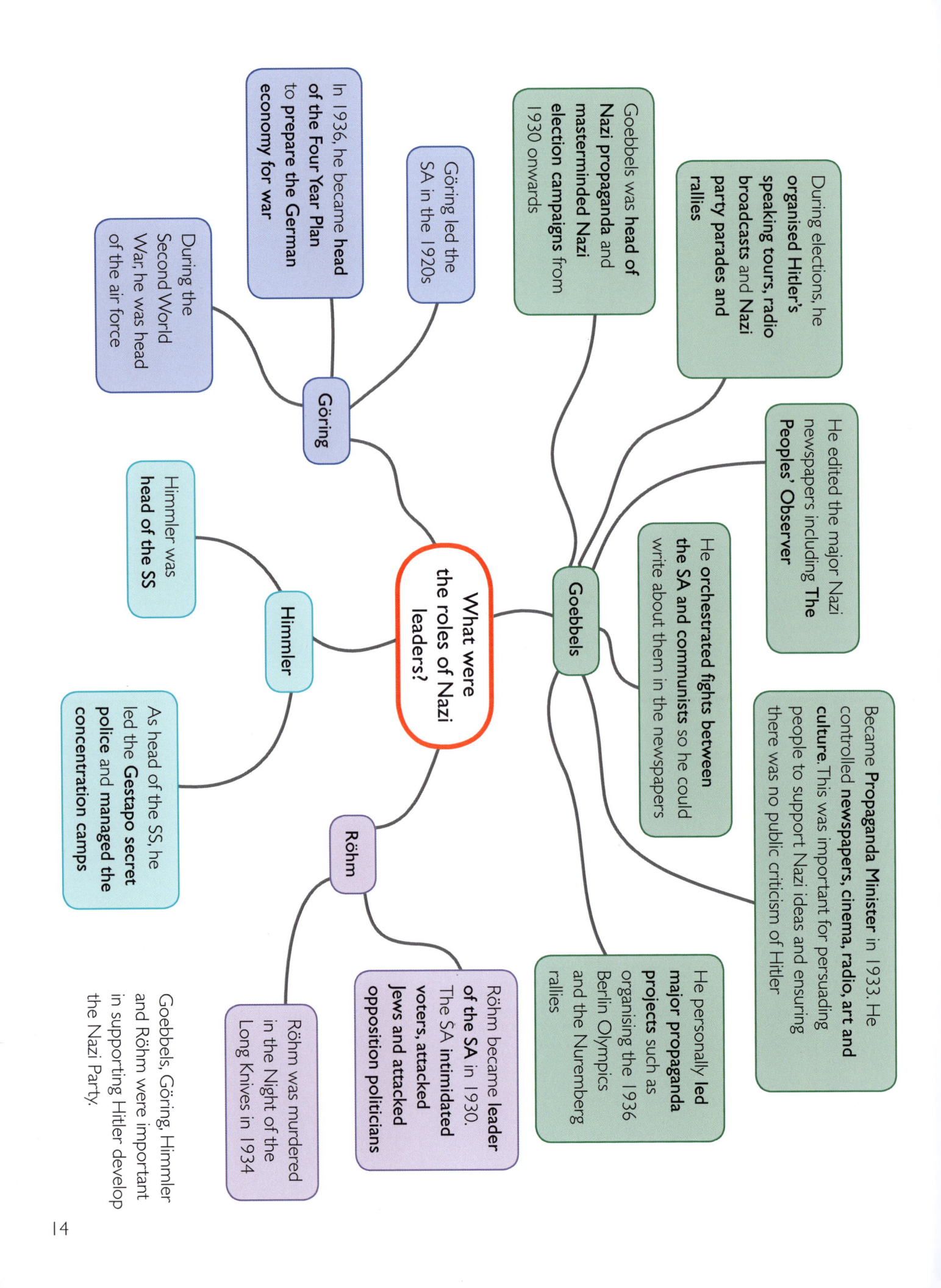

Göring

- Göring led the SA in the 1920s
- In 1936, he became head of the Four Year Plan to prepare the German economy for war
- During the Second World War, he was head of the air force

Goebbels

- Goebbels was head of Nazi propaganda and masterminded Nazi election campaigns from 1930 onwards
- During elections, he organised Hitler's speaking tours, radio broadcasts and Nazi party parades and rallies
- He edited the major Nazi newspapers including The Peoples' Observer
- Became **Propaganda Minister** in 1933. He controlled **newspapers, cinema, radio, art and culture**. This was important for persuading people to support Nazi ideas and ensuring there was no public criticism of Hitler
- He personally led major propaganda projects such as organising the 1936 Berlin Olympics and the Nuremberg rallies
- He orchestrated fights between **the SA and communists** so he could write about them in the newspapers

Himmler

- Himmler was **head of the SS**
- As head of the SS, he led the **Gestapo secret police** and managed the **concentration camps**

Röhm

- Röhm became leader of the SA in 1930. The SA **intimidated voters, attacked Jews and attacked opposition politicians**
- Röhm was murdered in the Night of the Long Knives in 1934

Goebbels, Göring, Himmler and Röhm were important in supporting Hitler develop the Nazi Party.

How did Hitler become Chancellor in 1933?

The Great Depression in 1929 caused severe economic problems for Germany. The extremists started to gain popularity again. President Hindenburg miscalculated by appointing Hitler as Chancellor. He thought Von Papen would be able to control him.

→ The Nazis lost support in the November 1932 elections. The party was running short of money to fund its activities

→ President Hindenburg wanted to appoint Von Papen as Chancellor, but Von Papen did not have enough seats to form a government on his own. He had to form a coalition with another party

→ Von Papen thought he could control Hitler in a coalition, so he asked Hindenburg to appoint Hitler as Chancellor with Von Papen serving as Vice Chancellor

→ Hindenburg appointed Hitler as Chancellor. The Nazis would hold 3 out of 12 Cabinet positions

→ Hitler probably would not have become Chancellor without Von Papen's need to form a coalition government and his help in persuading Hindenburg to appoint Hitler

What impact did the Great Depression have on the Weimar Republic? (3 Es)

Economic hardship

- **Unemployment rose to 6 million.** Many fell into poverty
- Economic problems were **blamed on the government**. People looked for **stronger government and leadership**
- **Chancellor Brüning cut wages for government jobs, raised taxes and reduced unemployment benefits.** This made the government unpopular. Opponents teased him with the slogan "Brüning Decrees Distress!"

Emergency powers

- Germany was **ruled by emergency decrees** using the President's Article 48 Powers
- Power became concentrated in the hands of the very old **President Hindenburg**, who seemed under the influence of the army and big business

Extremism

- Extremist propaganda offered people **scapegoats for economic problems**. Communists blamed industrialists, while Nazis blamed the Jews and Communists
- The Nazis and Communists **had radical solutions** to economic problems. These seemed attractive to many
- **Businessmen became worried about Communist success.** They started to support the Nazis
- **Nazi seats in the Reichstag grew:**
  - 1928 12 seats   (Before the depression)
  - 1930 107 seats   (After the depression)
  - 1932 230 seats   (Became the largest party in the Reichstag)

15

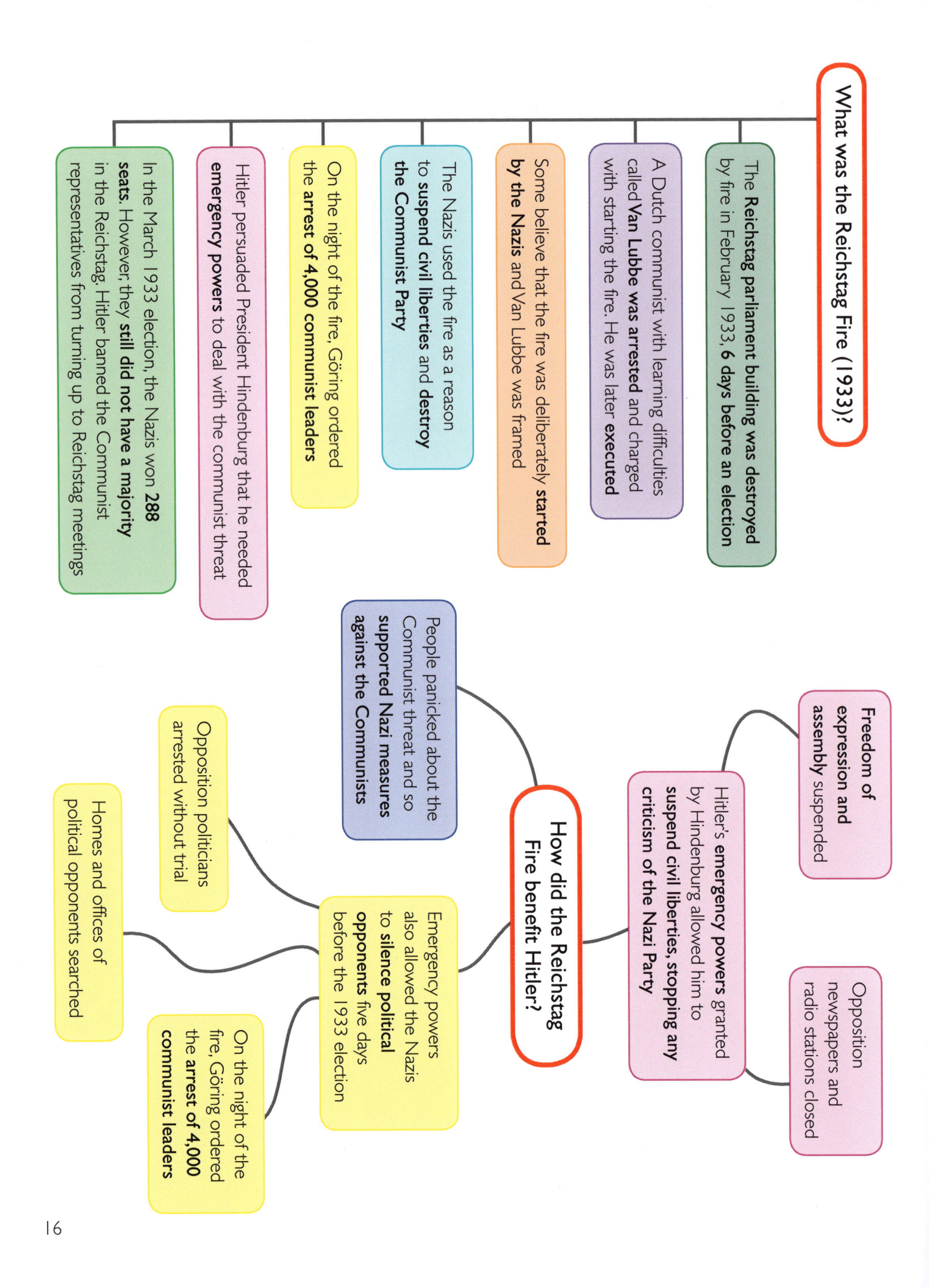

What was the Reichstag Fire (1933)?

- The **Reichstag** parliament building was destroyed by fire in February 1933, **6 days before an election**
- A Dutch communist with learning difficulties called **Van Lubbe was arrested** and charged with starting the fire. He was later **executed**
- Some believe that the fire was deliberately **started by the Nazis** and Van Lubbe was framed
- The Nazis used the fire as a reason to **suspend civil liberties** and **destroy the Communist Party**
- On the night of the fire, Göring ordered the **arrest of 4,000 communist leaders**
- Hitler persuaded President Hindenburg that he needed **emergency powers** to deal with the communist threat
- In the March 1933 election, the Nazis won **288 seats**. However, they **still did not have a majority** in the Reichstag. Hitler banned the Communist representatives from turning up to Reichstag meetings

How did the Reichstag Fire benefit Hitler?

- People panicked about the Communist threat and so **supported Nazi measures against the Communists**
- Hitler's **emergency powers** granted by Hindenburg allowed him to **suspend civil liberties**, stopping any **criticism of the Nazi Party**
  - Freedom of expression and assembly suspended
  - Opposition newspapers and radio stations closed
- Emergency powers also allowed the Nazis to **silence political opponents** five days before the 1933 election
  - Opposition politicians arrested without trial
  - Homes and offices of political opponents searched
- On the night of the fire, Göring ordered the **arrest of 4,000 communist leaders**

Why did Hitler become Chancellor in 1933? Part 1 (CHILI PEPPER)

Hindenburg

- President Hindenburg did not fully support the Weimar Republic. He only ran for President after receiving permission from the old Kaiser
- Hindenburg lacked the energy to stand up to the Nazis. He was 82 years old in 1930 and some medical historians believe he was suffering from dementia
- It was President Hindenburg who appointed Hitler as Chancellor
- However, Hindenburg probably would not have had to invite Hitler to become Chancellor if Von Papen had been able to secure a majority in the Reichstag

Industrialists' support

- Wealthy businessmen like Gustav Krupp and Frederick Thysen began to support the Nazis because they were worried about the increasing success of the Communists. They feared losing their businesses
- Thysen gave 650,000 marks to the Nazi Party and urged Hindenburg to appoint Hitler as Chancellor
- However, industrialists gave to every party except for the Communists (not just the Nazis)
- Financial support was used to pay for expensive propaganda and ferry Hitler between speaking engagements by aeroplane

Constitution weaknesses

- Hitler's change of political strategy after 1924 exploited weaknesses in the Weimar Constitution. Proportional representation allowed the Nazis to slowly build up Reichstag seats
- The Social Democrats were the largest party in the Reichstag in 1930, but held only 24.5% of the seats. A total of 14 different political parties held seats
- Political decisions required compromise between lots of different parties
- Proportional representation prevented strong, single party governments
- Von Papen could not form a government on his own without entering a coalition government with the Nazis
- Government weaknesses prevented decisive action to address the economic collapse. Some Germans thought a dictatorship would offer more stable, stronger government

Long term problems with the Weimar Republic

- Repeated failures, such as hyperinflation and failure to deal with the economic depression, left many disillusioned with the Republic and looking for alternatives
- Many had never supported the Republic. In 1918, many would have preferred the return of the Kaiser or a Communist revolution
- The Weimar Republic remained associated with the defeat of the First World War and humiliation of the Versailles Treaty. Hitler's calls to abolish the treaty appealed to many

17

Why did Hitler become Chancellor in 1933? Part 2 (CHILI PEPPER)

Intimidation

- SA stormtroopers demonstrated outside polling stations, handed out leaflets and intimidated voters
- SA guarded Hitler's speaking engagements, ensuring that he was not interrupted
- The SA fought the Communist Red Front on the streets. Berlin court cases involving **political violence rose from 50 in 1931 to 311 in 1933**. This **raised fear of Communism**
- However, propaganda was required to ensure that the Communists and not the SA were blamed for political violence. Also, the SA was relatively small before the economic collapse (60,000 members in 1930 and 471,000 in 1932)

Personality of Hitler

- Hitler was a **strong, determined and ruthless leader**. Nazi propaganda built a myth of Hitler as a supremely able leader capable of transforming Germany
- Hitler was a particularly persuasive orator. The Nazis **flew him around the country during election campaigns** making speeches. In the 1932 election campaign, Hitler spoke in 12 major cities in 11 days with audiences numbering up to 25,000

Propaganda

- Rallies, parades and marches gave people a **sense of togetherness** and belonging to a national movement
- Posters used simple and clear messages appealing to people's **basic fears and desires**. Some promised "bread and work". Others stressed Hitler's strong leadership

Economic depression

- The Weimar government did not seem to have solutions. **Chancellor Brüning** made the situation worse by raising taxes, decreasing unemployment benefits and cutting wages for government jobs
- The Great Depression hit Germany particularly badly. It left **6 million unemployed and many in poverty**
- The Nazis **offered radical solutions**. Germans turned to them because they were **desperate**
- Nazi propaganda promised **"work and bread"** and blamed **Jews and Communists** for the economic situation

Popular policies

- Nazi policies appealed to many who were suffering during the Depression. They appealed to basic needs and fears
- The Nazis **seemed to offer solutions** to unemployment and economic problems. Hitler promised to make Germany a great power again
- The Nazis were **flexible in their policies. Unpopular policies were quickly dropped.** In the 1920s, the Nazis wanted to take ownership of businesses away from industrialists, but the Nazis needed funding from rich businessmen to get elected

18

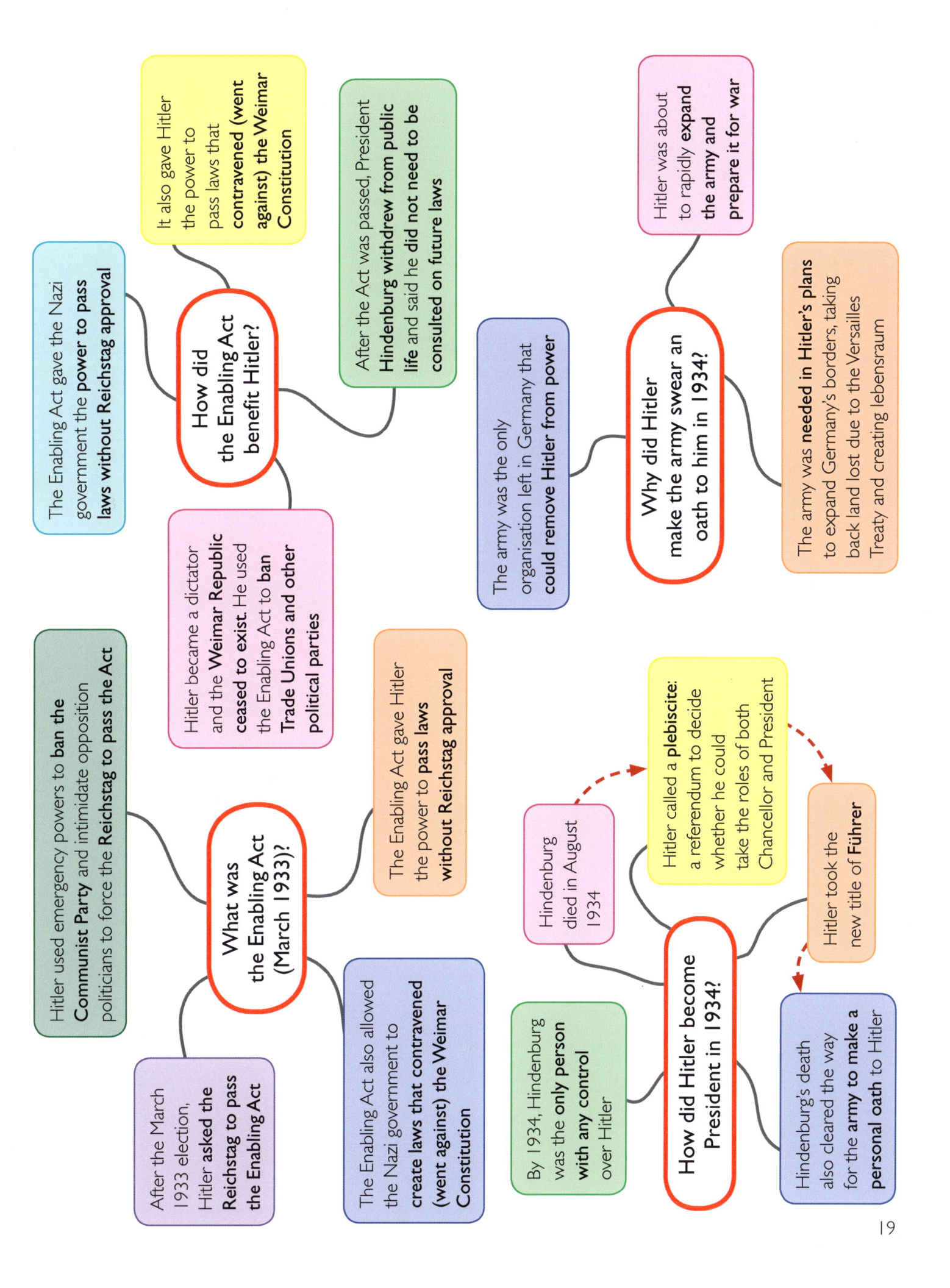

How did the Enabling Act benefit Hitler?

- The Enabling Act gave the Nazi government the power to pass laws without Reichstag approval
- It also gave Hitler the power to pass laws that contravened (went against) the Weimar Constitution
- After the Act was passed, President Hindenburg withdrew from public life and said he did not need to be consulted on future laws
- Hitler became a dictator and the Weimar Republic ceased to exist. He used the Enabling Act to ban Trade Unions and other political parties

What was the Enabling Act (March 1933)?

- Hitler used emergency powers to ban the Communist Party and intimidate opposition politicians to force the Reichstag to pass the Act
- After the March 1933 election, Hitler asked the Reichstag to pass the Enabling Act
- The Enabling Act gave Hitler the power to pass laws without Reichstag approval
- The Enabling Act also allowed the Nazi government to create laws that contravened (went against) the Weimar Constitution

Why did Hitler make the army swear an oath to him in 1934?

- Hitler was about to rapidly expand the army and prepare it for war
- The army was needed in Hitler's plans to expand Germany's borders, taking back land lost due to the Versailles Treaty and creating lebensraum
- The army was the only organisation left in Germany that could remove Hitler from power

How did Hitler become President in 1934?

- Hindenburg died in August 1934
- Hitler called a plebiscite: a referendum to decide whether he could take the roles of both Chancellor and President
- Hitler took the new title of Führer
- Hindenburg's death also cleared the way for the army to make a personal oath to Hitler
- By 1934, Hindenburg was the only person with any control over Hitler

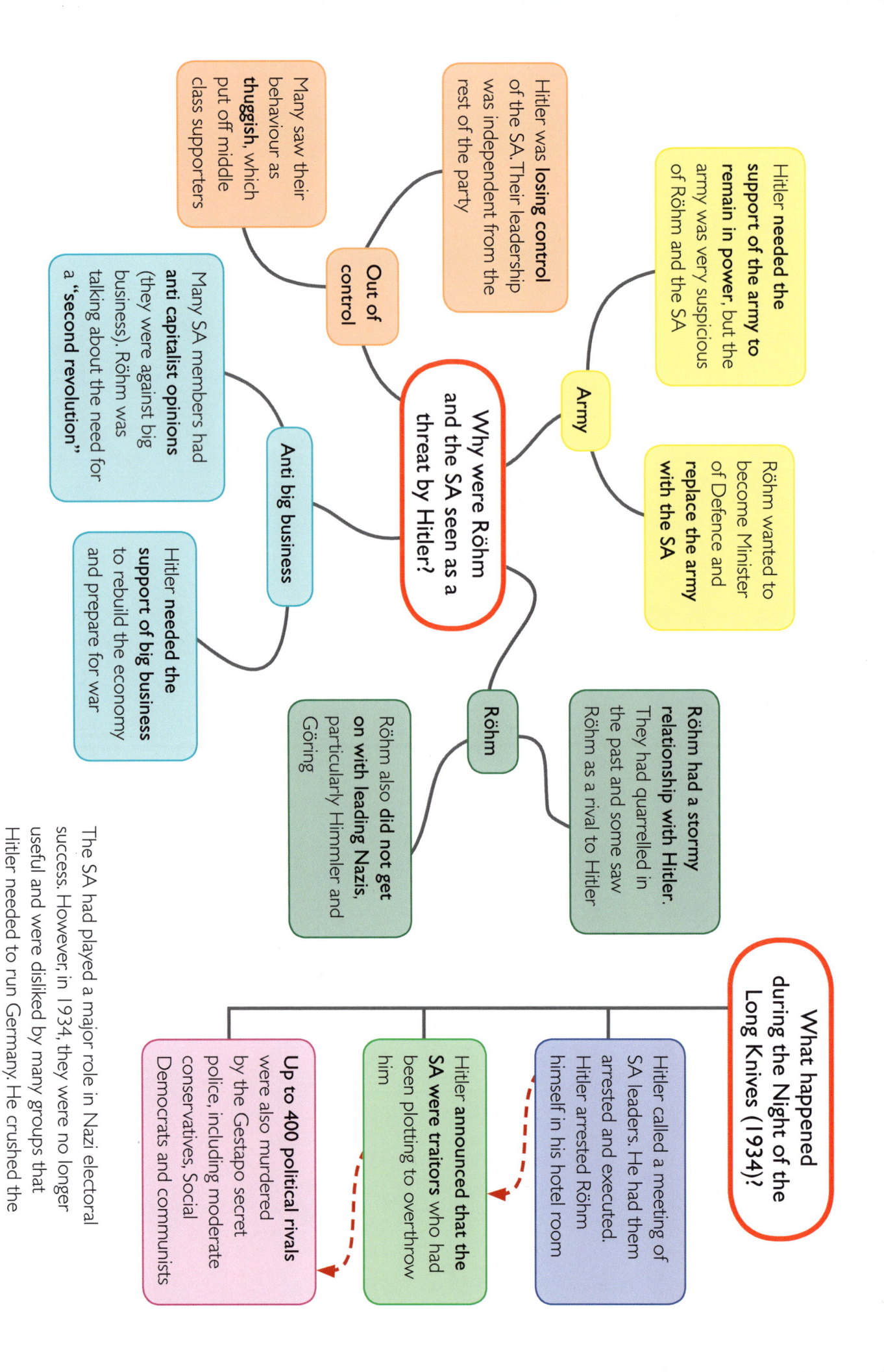

Why were Röhm and the SA seen as a threat by Hitler?

Army

- Hitler needed the support of the army to **remain in power**, but the army was very suspicious of Röhm and the SA
- Röhm wanted to become Minister of Defence and **replace the army with the SA**

Out of control

- Hitler was **losing control** of the SA. Their leadership was independent from the rest of the party
- Many saw their behaviour as **thuggish**, which put off middle class supporters

Anti big business

- Many SA members had **anti capitalist opinions** (they were against big business). Röhm was talking about the need for a **"second revolution"**
- Hitler needed the **support of big business** to rebuild the economy and prepare for war

Röhm

- Röhm had a stormy **relationship with Hitler**. They had quarrelled in the past and some saw Röhm as a rival to Hitler
- Röhm also **did not get on with leading Nazis**, particularly Himmler and Göring

What happened during the Night of the Long Knives (1934)?

- Hitler called a meeting of SA leaders. He had them arrested and executed. Hitler arrested Röhm himself in his hotel room
- Hitler announced that the **SA were traitors** who had been plotting to overthrow him
- Up to **400 political rivals** were also murdered by the Gestapo secret police, including moderate conservatives, Social Democrats and communists

The SA had played a major role in Nazi electoral success. However, in 1934, they were no longer useful and were disliked by many groups that Hitler needed to run Germany. He crushed the organisation in the Night of the Long Knives.

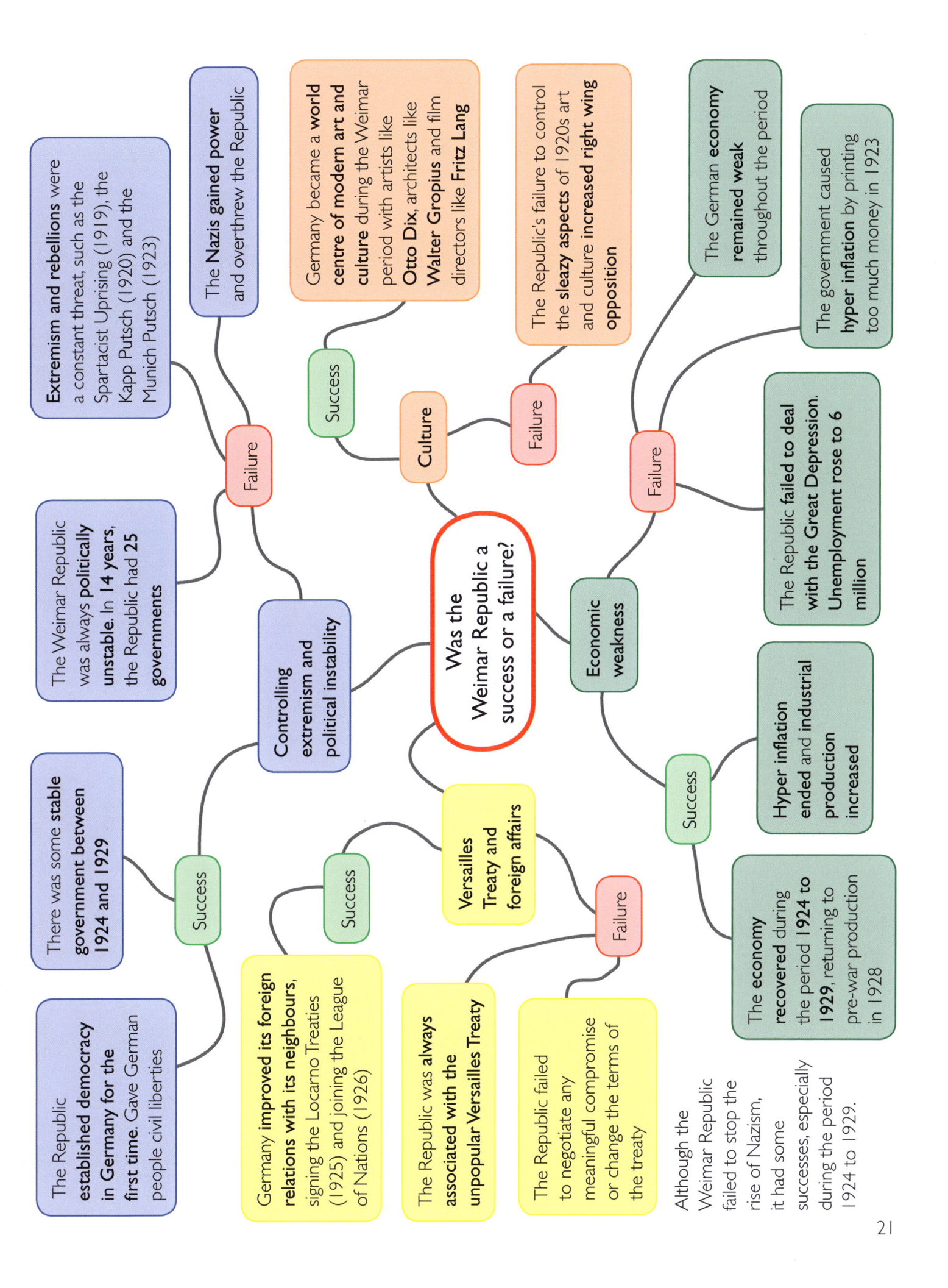

Was the Weimar Republic a success or a failure?

Controlling extremism and political instability

Failure:
- Extremism and rebellions were a constant threat, such as the Spartacist Uprising (1919), the Kapp Putsch (1920) and the Munich Putsch (1923)
- The Nazis gained power and overthrew the Republic
- The Weimar Republic was always politically unstable. In 14 years, the Republic had 25 governments

Success:
- There was some stable government between 1924 and 1929
- The Republic established democracy in Germany for the first time. Gave German people civil liberties

Culture

Success:
- Germany became a world centre of modern art and culture during the Weimar period with artists like Otto Dix, architects like Walter Gropius and film directors like Fritz Lang

Failure:
- The Republic's failure to control the sleazy aspects of 1920s art and culture increased right wing opposition

Economic weakness

Failure:
- The German economy remained weak throughout the period
- The government caused hyper inflation by printing too much money in 1923
- The Republic failed to deal with the Great Depression. Unemployment rose to 6 million

Success:
- Hyper inflation ended and industrial production increased
- The economy recovered during the period 1924 to 1929, returning to pre-war production in 1928

Versailles Treaty and foreign affairs

Success:
- Germany improved its foreign relations with its neighbours, signing the Locarno Treaties (1925) and joining the League of Nations (1926)

Failure:
- The Republic was always associated with the unpopular Versailles Treaty
- The Republic failed to negotiate any meaningful compromise or change the terms of the treaty

Although the Weimar Republic failed to stop the rise of Nazism, it had some successes, especially during the period 1924 to 1929.

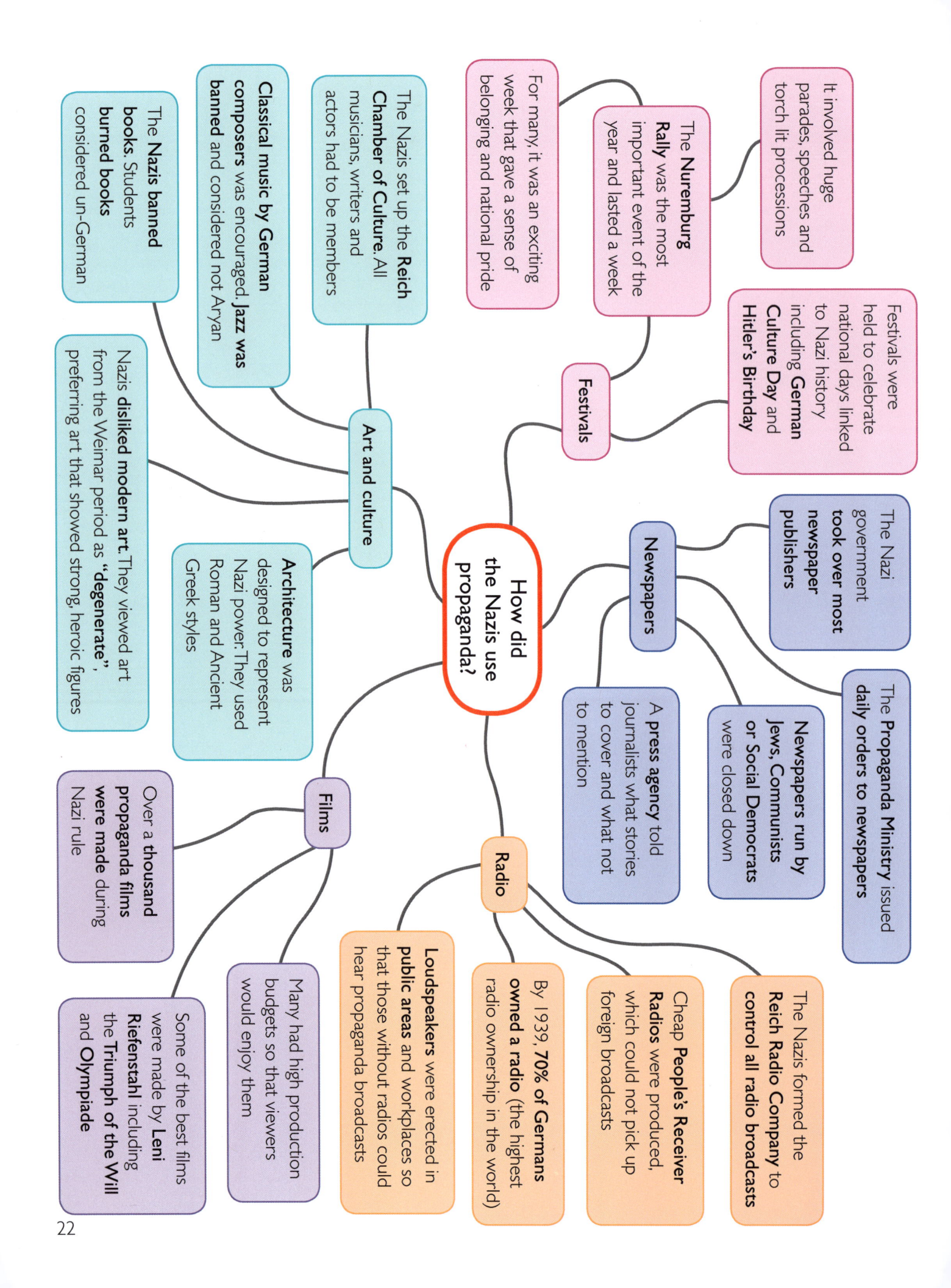

How did the Nazis use propaganda?

Festivals

- The **Nuremburg Rally** was the most important event of the year and lasted a week
- It involved huge parades, speeches and torch lit processions
- For many, it was an exciting week that gave a sense of belonging and national pride
- Festivals were held to celebrate national days linked to Nazi history including **German Culture Day** and **Hitler's Birthday**

Art and culture

- The Nazis set up the **Reich Chamber of Culture**. All musicians, writers and actors had to be members
- Classical music by German composers was encouraged. **Jazz was banned** and considered not Aryan
- The **Nazis banned books**. Students **burned books** considered un-German
- Nazis disliked modern art. They viewed art from the Weimar period as "degenerate", preferring art that showed strong, heroic figures
- **Architecture** was designed to represent Nazi power. They used Roman and Ancient Greek styles

Newspapers

- The Nazi government took over most newspaper publishers
- The Propaganda Ministry issued daily orders to newspapers
- Newspapers run by **Jews, Communists or Social Democrats** were closed down
- A press agency told journalists what stories to cover and what not to mention

Radio

- The Nazis formed the **Reich Radio Company** to control all radio broadcasts
- Cheap **People's Receiver Radios** were produced, which could not pick up foreign broadcasts
- By 1939, **70% of Germans owned a radio** (the highest radio ownership in the world)
- **Loudspeakers** were erected in **public areas** and workplaces so that those without radios could hear propaganda broadcasts

Films

- Over a **thousand propaganda films were made** during Nazi rule
- Many had high production budgets so that viewers would enjoy them
- Some of the best films were made by **Leni Riefenstahl** including the **Triumph of the Will** and **Olympiade**

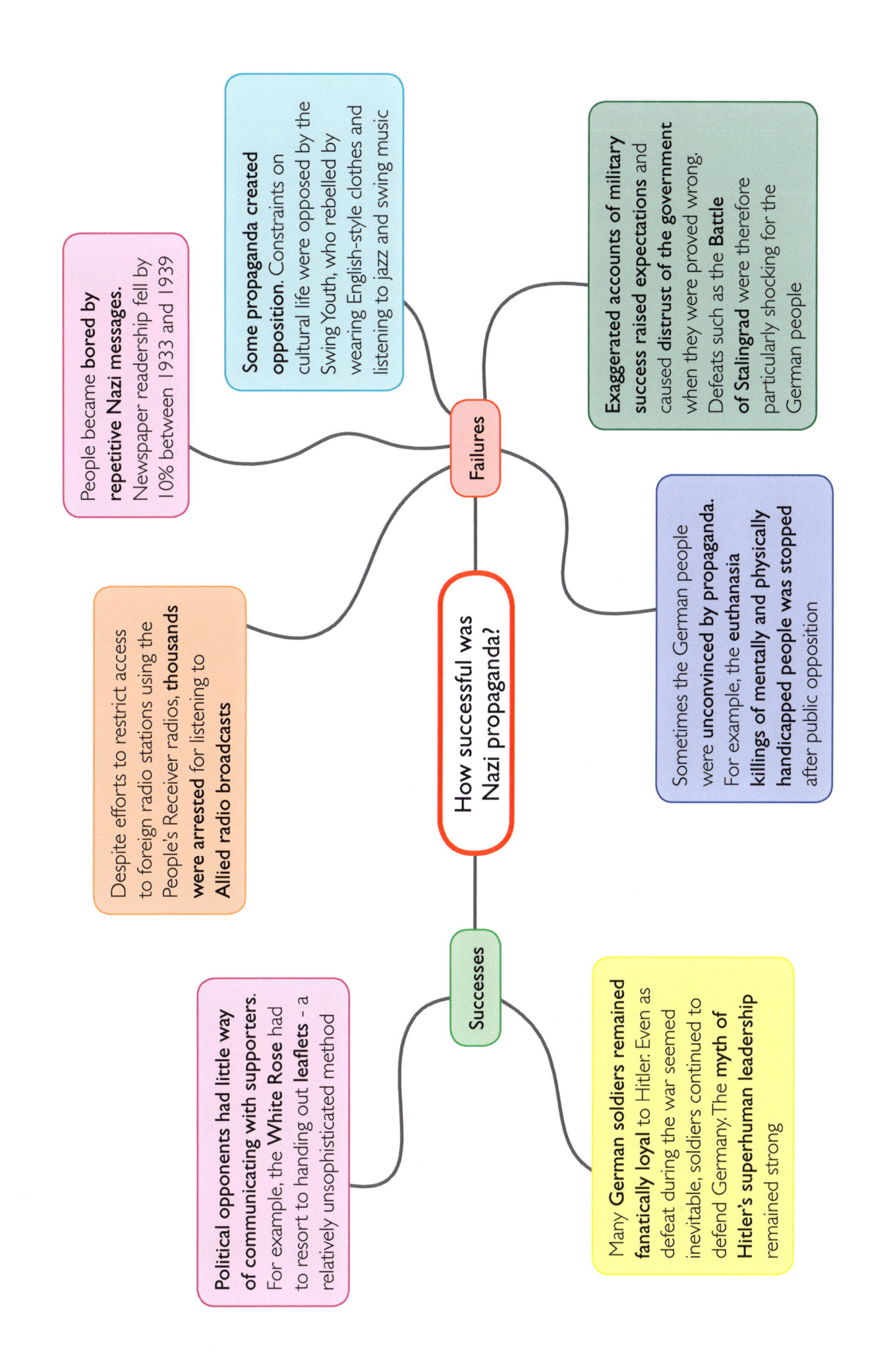

How successful was Nazi propaganda?

Failures

- **People became bored by repetitive Nazi messages.** Newspaper readership fell by 10% between 1933 and 1939

- **Some propaganda created opposition.** Constraints on cultural life were opposed by the Swing Youth, who rebelled by wearing English-style clothes and listening to jazz and swing music

- **Exaggerated accounts of military success raised expectations** and caused distrust of the government when they were proved wrong. Defeats such as the **Battle of Stalingrad** were therefore particularly shocking for the German people

- Sometimes the German people were unconvinced by propaganda. For example, the euthanasia **killings of mentally and physically handicapped people was stopped** after public opposition

- Despite efforts to restrict access to foreign radio stations using the People's Receiver radios, **thousands were arrested** for listening to Allied radio broadcasts

Successes

- **Political opponents had little way of communicating with supporters.** For example, the **White Rose** had to resort to handing out **leaflets** - a relatively unsophisticated method

- Many **German soldiers remained fanatically loyal** to Hitler. Even as defeat during the war seemed inevitable, soldiers continued to defend Germany. The **myth of Hitler's superhuman leadership** remained strong

What was the role of the SS and Gestapo? What were concentration camps?

What were concentration camps?

- **At first**, the camps held **political critics** of the Nazis such as Communists, Social Democrats and trade unionists
- Later they held **Jews, homosexuals and other groups persecuted** by the Nazis
- Prisoners did **hard labour** in quarries, agriculture or forestry. Later, the camps were used to **exterminate prisoners in gas chambers**
- Food was limited and prisoners suffered **harsh discipline, physical assaults** and **random executions**

How did the Gestapo control the German people?

- Those who plotted against the Nazis, for example soldiers involved in the July 1945 assassination plot or members of the White Rose opposition group, were **arrested and executed by the Gestapo**
- They investigated and punished cases of **treason, espionage, sabotage** and **political opposition**
- The Gestapo had almost **unlimited powers of arrest and detention**
- They had a **network of informers**. Ordinary people were encouraged to **inform on their neighbours**
- The Gestapo was **greatly feared** by ordinary Germans. As a result, many were too afraid to challenge Nazi rule
- The Gestapo was a **secret police** unit

What was the SS?

- The SS was originally Hitler's **personal bodyguard**
- By 1936, its role had widened to include **secret police, fighting units** and groups **managing concentration camps**
- They helped destroy **the SA** during the Night of the Long Knives (1934)
- The **Gestapo** was part of the SS

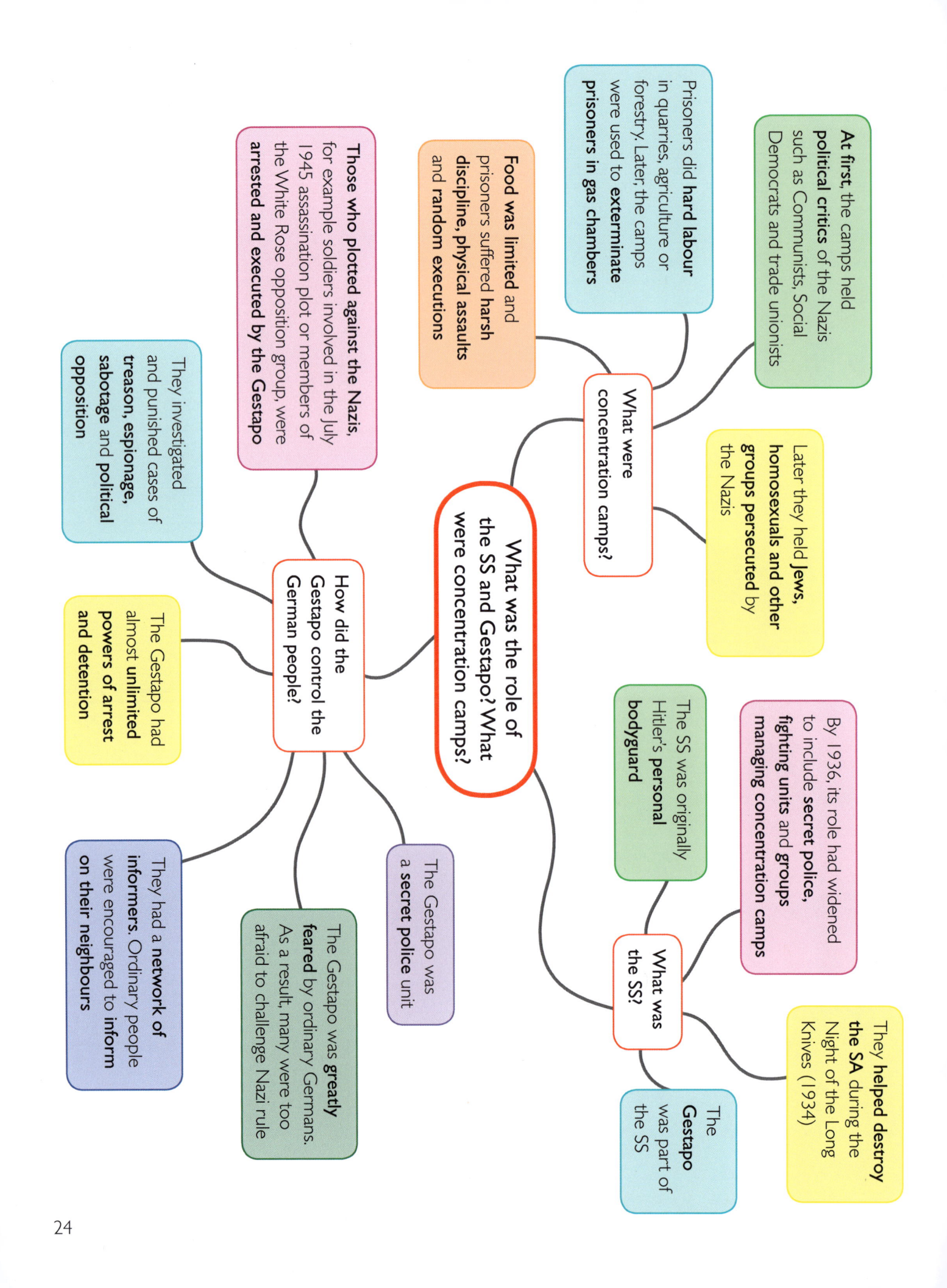

24

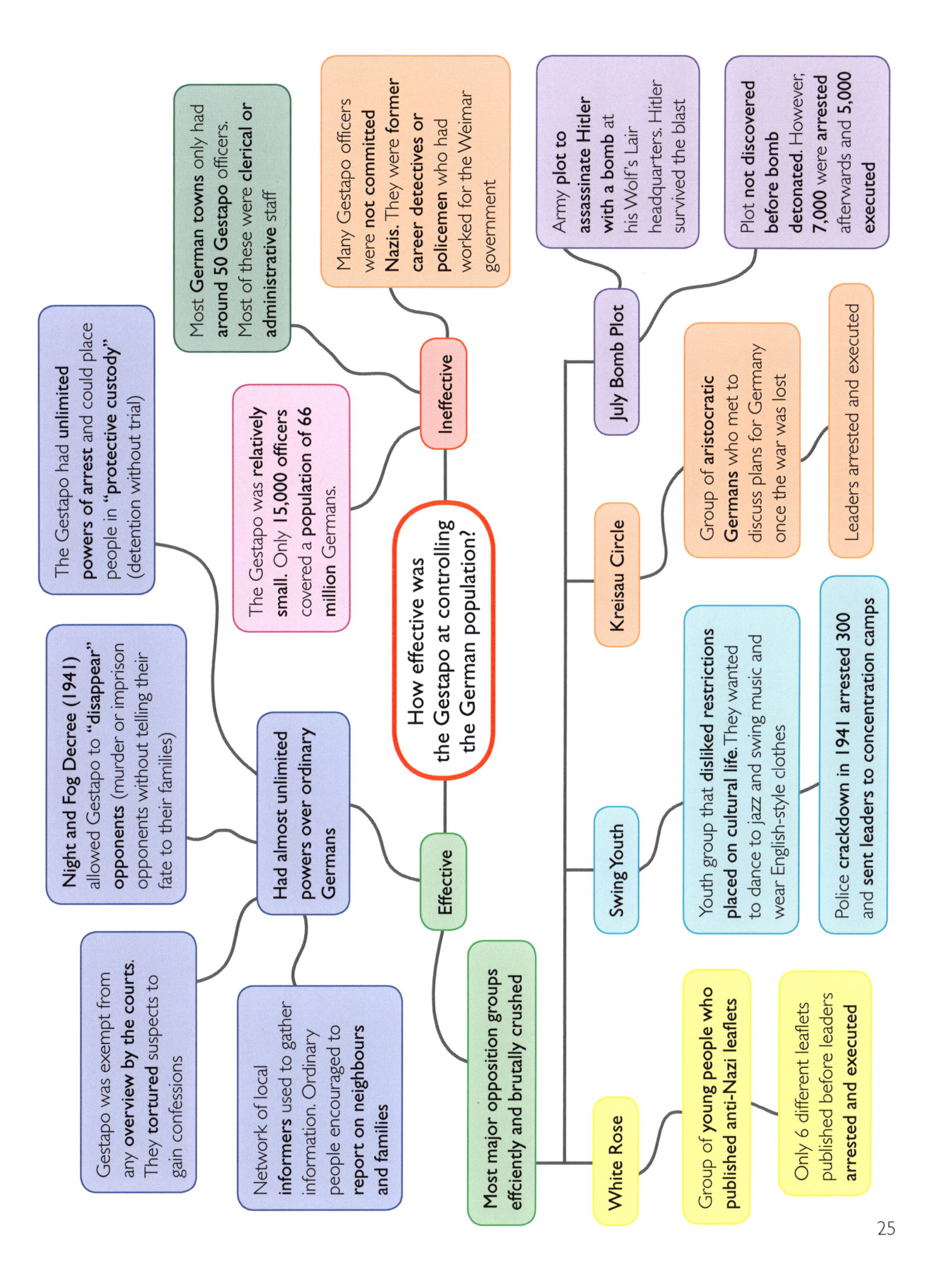

How effective was the Gestapo at controlling the German population?

Ineffective

- Most German towns only had **around 50 Gestapo** officers. Most of these were **clerical or administrative staff**
- Many Gestapo officers were **not committed Nazis**. They were former **career detectives or policemen** who had worked for the Weimar government
- The Gestapo was relatively small. Only **15,000 officers** covered a **population of 66 million Germans**.

Effective

- The Gestapo had **unlimited powers of arrest** and could place people in **"protective custody"** (detention without trial)
- **Night and Fog Decree (1941)** allowed Gestapo to **"disappear" opponents** (murder or imprison opponents without telling their fate to their families)
- Gestapo was exempt from any **overview by the courts**. They **tortured** suspects to gain confessions
- Network of local **informers** used to gather information. Ordinary people encouraged to **report on neighbours and families**
- Had almost unlimited powers over ordinary Germans
- Most major opposition groups efficiently and brutally crushed

July Bomb Plot
- Army plot to assassinate Hitler with a bomb at his Wolf's Lair headquarters. Hitler survived the blast
- Plot not discovered before bomb detonated. However, **7,000 were arrested** afterwards and **5,000 executed**

Kreisau Circle
- Group of **aristocratic Germans** who met to discuss plans for Germany once the war was lost
- Leaders arrested and executed

Swing Youth
- Youth group that disliked restrictions placed on cultural life. They wanted to dance to jazz and swing music and wear English-style clothes
- Police crackdown in 1941 arrested 300 and sent leaders to concentration camps

White Rose
- Group of **young people who published anti-Nazi leaflets**
- Only 6 different leaflets published before leaders **arrested and executed**

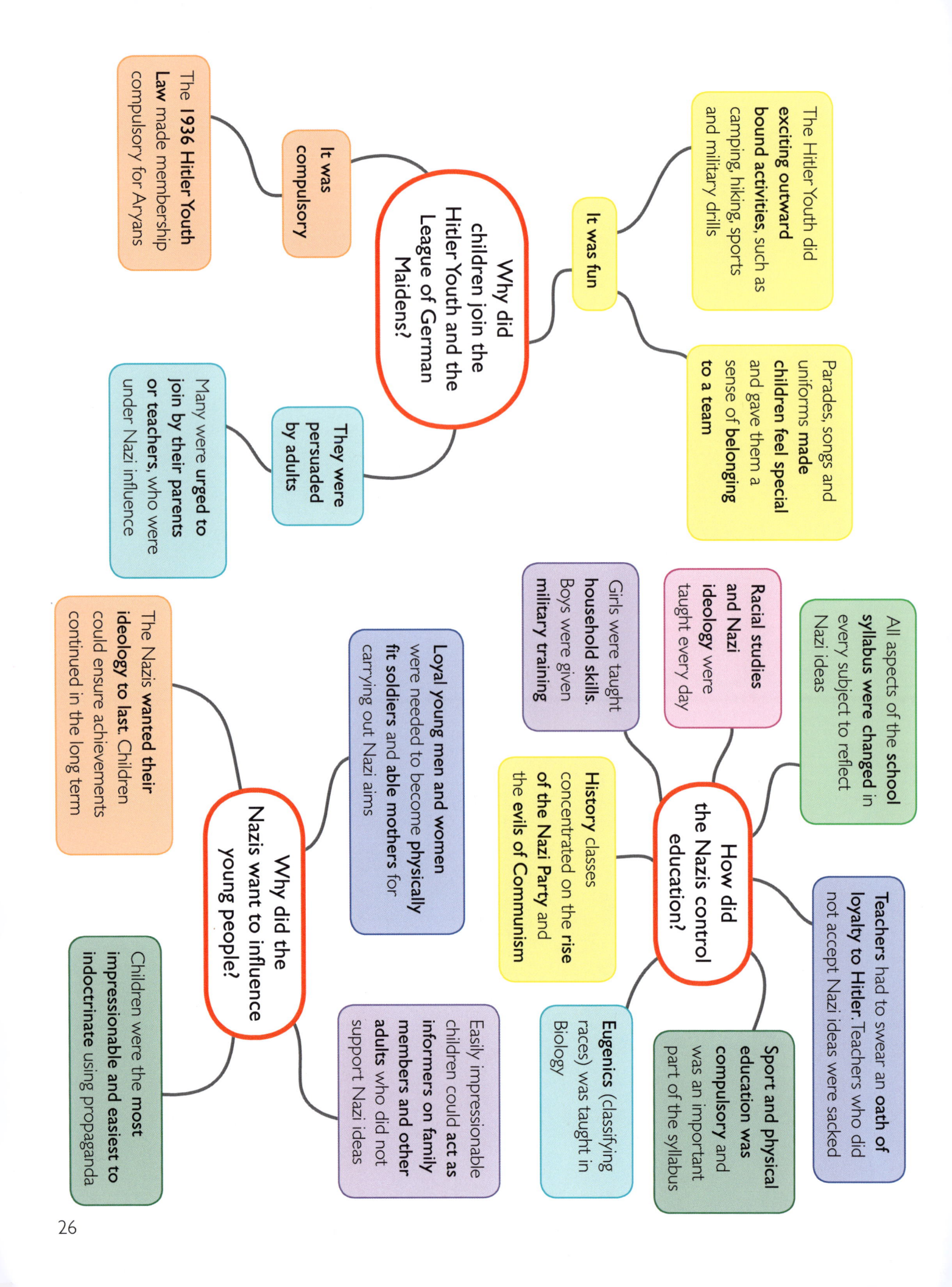

Why did children join the Hitler Youth and the League of German Maidens?

It was compulsory
- The 1936 Hitler Youth Law made membership compulsory for Aryans

It was fun
- The Hitler Youth did exciting outward bound activities, such as camping, hiking sports and military drills
- Parades, songs and uniforms made children feel special and gave them a sense of belonging to a team

They were persuaded by adults
- Many were urged to join by their parents or teachers, who were under Nazi influence

How did the Nazis control education?

- All aspects of the school syllabus were changed in every subject to reflect Nazi ideas
- Racial studies and Nazi ideology were taught every day
- Girls were taught household skills. Boys were given military training
- History classes concentrated on the rise of the Nazi Party and the evils of Communism
- Eugenics (classifying races) was taught in Biology
- Sport and physical education was compulsory and was an important part of the syllabus
- Teachers had to swear an oath of loyalty to Hitler. Teachers who did not accept Nazi ideas were sacked

Why did the Nazis want to influence young people?

- The Nazis wanted their ideology to last. Children could ensure achievements continued in the long term
- Loyal young men and women were needed to become physically fit soldiers and able mothers for carrying out Nazi aims
- Easily impressionable children could act as informers on family members and other adults who did not support Nazi ideas
- Children were the most impressionable and easiest to indoctrinate using propaganda

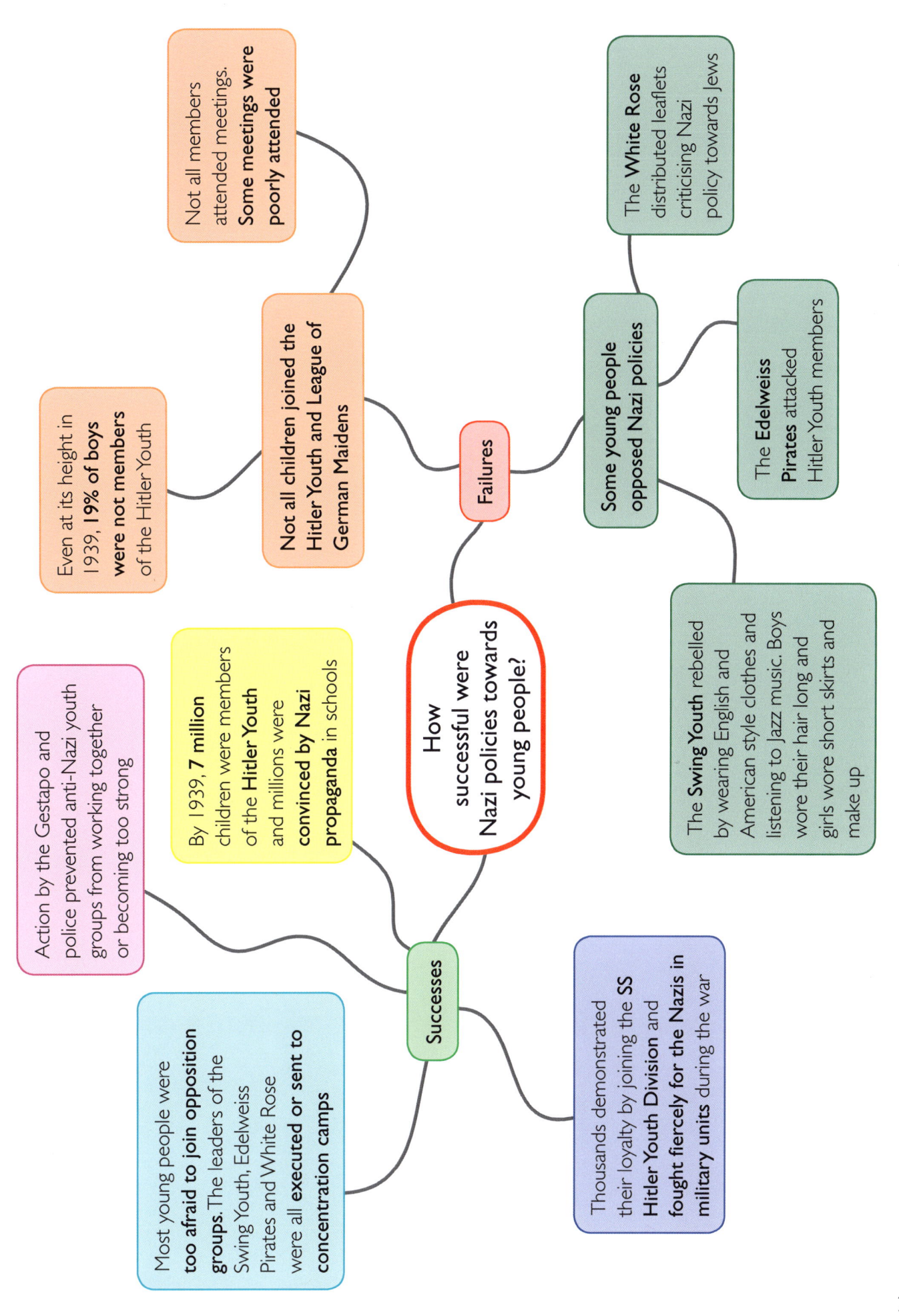

How successful were Nazi policies towards young people?

Failures

- Not all members attended meetings. **Some meetings were poorly attended**
- Even at its height in 1939, **19% of boys were not members** of the Hitler Youth
- **Not all children joined the Hitler Youth and League of German Maidens**
- **Some young people opposed Nazi policies**
  - The **White Rose** distributed leaflets criticising Nazi policy towards Jews
  - The **Edelweiss Pirates** attacked Hitler Youth members
  - The **Swing Youth** rebelled by wearing English and American style clothes and listening to Jazz music. Boys wore their hair long and girls wore short skirts and make up

Successes

- Action by the Gestapo and police prevented anti-Nazi youth groups from working together or becoming too strong
- By 1939, **7 million** children were members of the **Hitler Youth** and millions were **convinced by Nazi propaganda** in schools
- Most young people were **too afraid to join opposition groups**. The leaders of the Swing Youth, Edelweiss Pirates and White Rose were all executed or sent to concentration camps
- Thousands demonstrated their loyalty by joining the **SS Hitler Youth Division and fought fiercely for the Nazis in military units** during the war

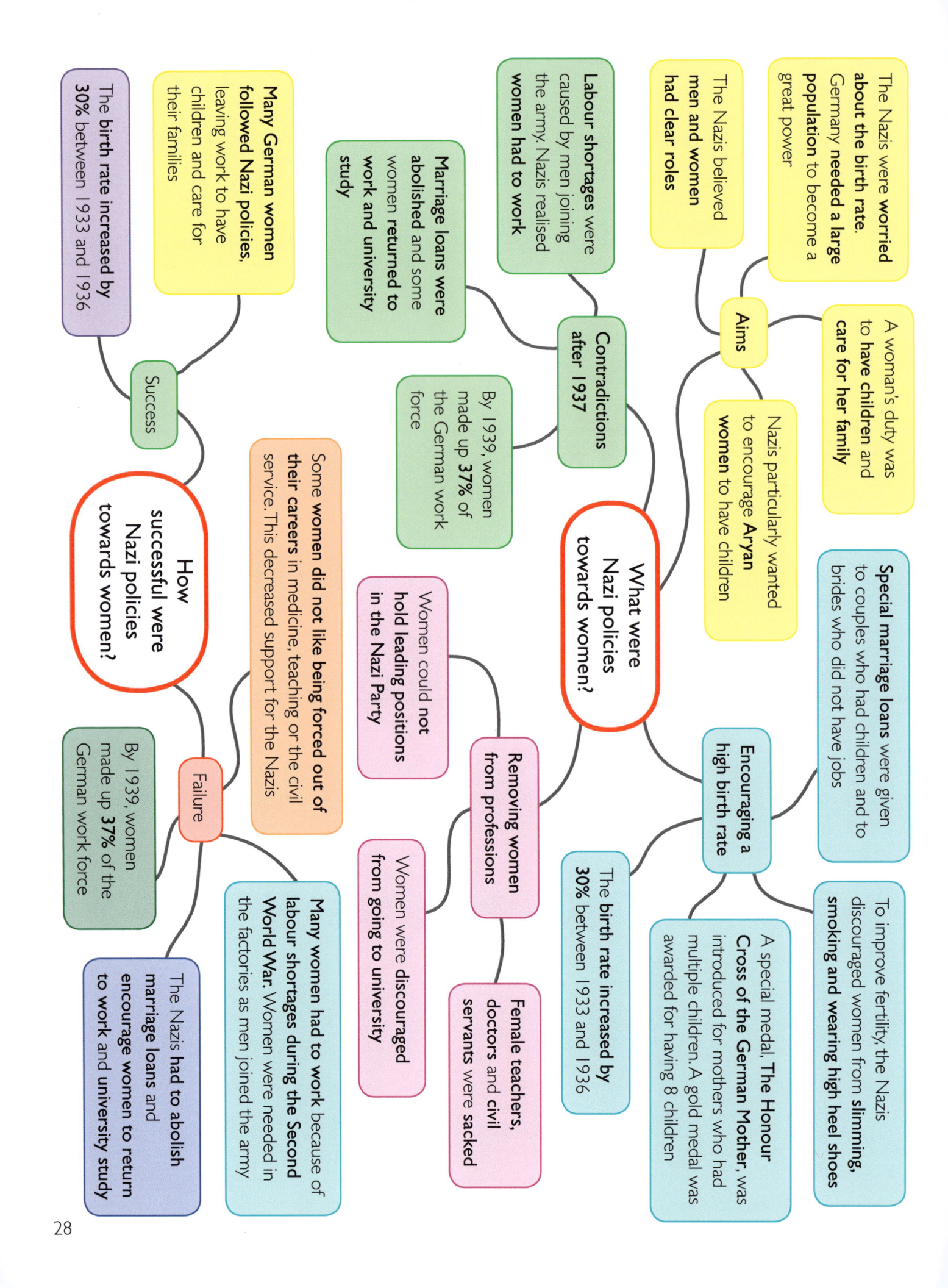

What were Nazi policies towards women?

Aims

- The Nazis were worried about the birth rate. Germany needed a large population to become a great power
- The Nazis believed men and women had clear roles
- A woman's duty was to have children and care for her family
- Nazis particularly wanted to encourage **Aryan women** to have children

Encouraging a high birth rate

- Special marriage loans were given to couples who had children and to brides who did not have jobs
- To improve fertility, the Nazis discouraged women from **slimming, smoking and wearing high heel shoes**
- A special medal, **The Honour Cross of the German Mother**, was introduced for mothers who had multiple children. A gold medal was awarded for having 8 children
- The **birth rate increased by 30%** between 1933 and 1936

Removing women from professions

- Female teachers, doctors and civil servants were sacked
- Women were discouraged from going to university
- Women could not hold leading positions in the Nazi Party

Contradictions after 1937

- Labour shortages were caused by men joining the army. Nazis realised **women had to work**
- Marriage loans were abolished and some women returned to **work and university study**
- By 1939, women made up **37%** of the German work force

How successful were Nazi policies towards women?

Success

- Many German women followed Nazi policies, leaving work to have children and care for their families
- The birth rate increased by **30%** between 1933 and 1936

Failure

- Some **women did not like being forced out of their careers** in medicine, teaching or the civil service. This decreased support for the Nazis
- By 1939, women made up **37%** of the German work force
- Many women had to work because of labour shortages during the Second World War. Women were needed in the factories as men joined the army
- The Nazis **had to abolish marriage loans and encourage women to return to work and university study**

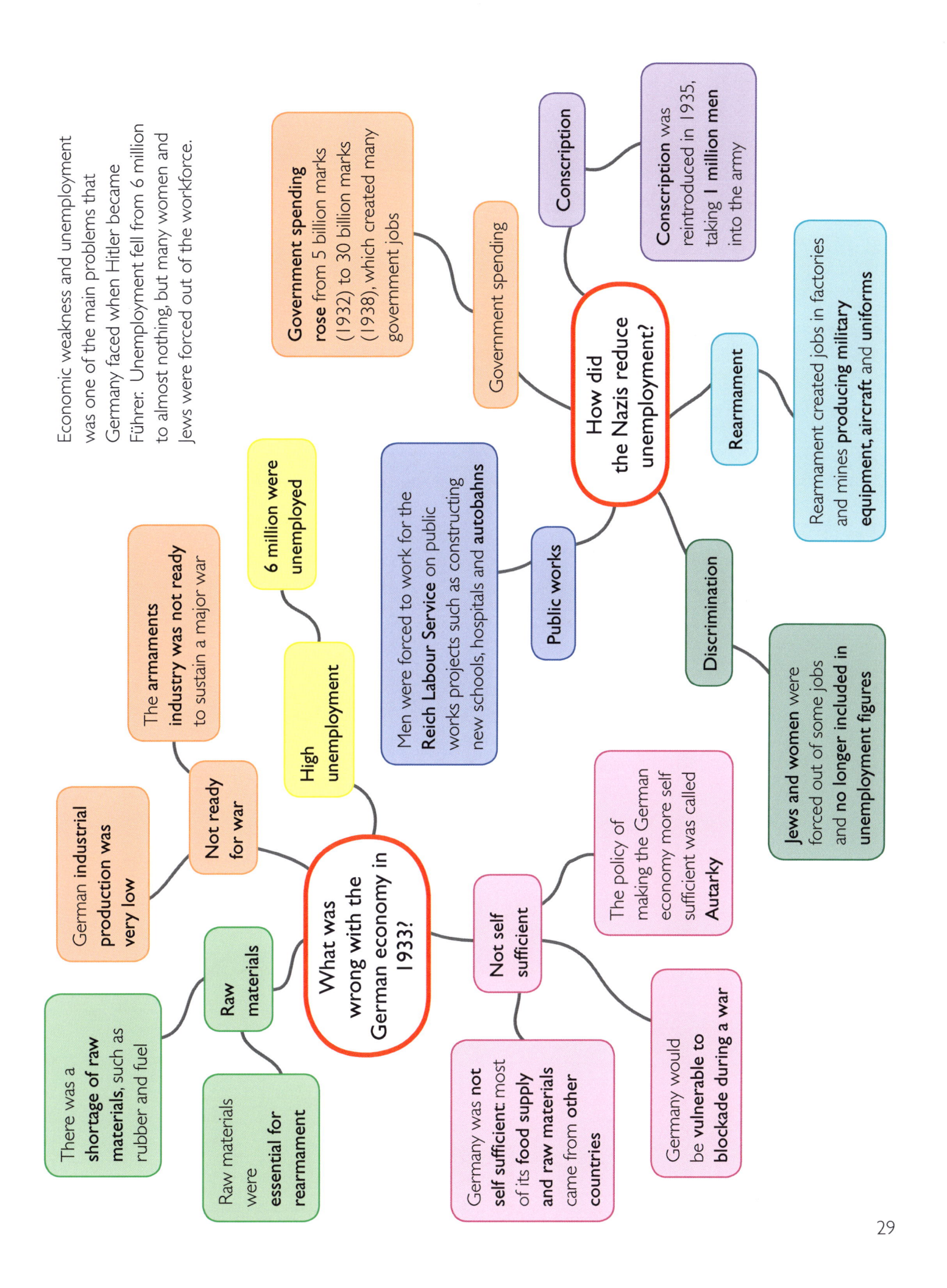

Economic weakness and unemployment was one of the main problems that Germany faced when Hitler became Führer. Unemployment fell from 6 million to almost nothing, but many women and Jews were forced out of the workforce.

How did the Nazis reduce unemployment?

Government spending
- **Government spending rose** from 5 billion marks (1932) to 30 billion marks (1938), which created many government jobs

Conscription
- **Conscription** was reintroduced in 1935, taking 1 million men into the army

Rearmament
- Rearmament created jobs in factories and mines **producing military equipment, aircraft and uniforms**

Public works
- Men were forced to work for the **Reich Labour Service** on public works projects such as constructing new schools, hospitals and **autobahns**

Discrimination
- **Jews and women** were forced out of some jobs and no longer included in unemployment figures

What was wrong with the German economy in 1933?

High unemployment
- 6 million were unemployed

Not ready for war
- German **industrial production was very low**
- The armaments industry **was not ready to sustain a major war**

Raw materials
- There was a **shortage of raw materials**, such as rubber and fuel
- Raw materials were **essential for rearmament**

Not self sufficient
- The policy of making the German economy more self sufficient was called **Autarky**
- Germany was **not self sufficient**: most of its **food supply and raw materials** came from other countries
- Germany would be **vulnerable to blockade during a war**

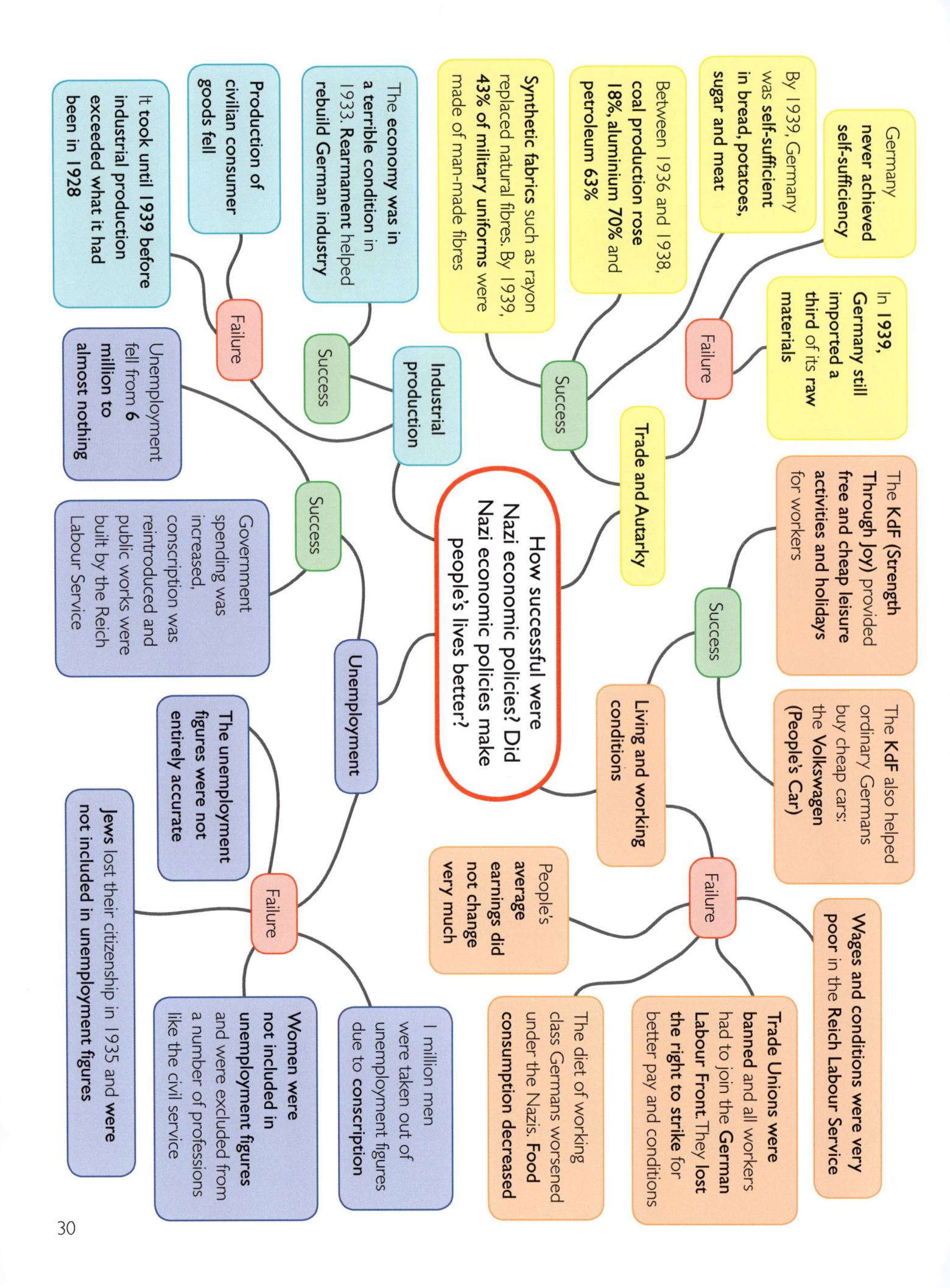

How successful were Nazi economic policies? Did Nazi economic policies make people's lives better?

Trade and Autarky

Success
- By 1939, Germany was self-sufficient in bread, potatoes, sugar and meat
- Between 1936 and 1938, coal production rose 18%, aluminium 70% and petroleum 63%
- Synthetic fabrics such as rayon replaced natural fibres. By 1939, 43% of military uniforms were made of man-made fibres

Failure
- Germany never achieved self-sufficiency
- In 1939, Germany still imported a third of its raw materials

Industrial production

Success
- The economy was in a terrible condition in 1933. Rearmament helped rebuild German industry
- It took until 1939 before industrial production exceeded what it had been in 1928

Failure
- Production of civilian consumer goods fell

Unemployment

Success
- Unemployment fell from 6 million to almost nothing
- Government spending was increased, conscription was reintroduced and public works were built by the Reich Labour Service

Failure
- The unemployment figures were not entirely accurate
- Jews lost their citizenship in 1935 and were not included in unemployment figures
- Women were not included in unemployment figures and were excluded from a number of professions like the civil service
- 1 million men were taken out of unemployment figures due to conscription

Living and working conditions

Success
- The KdF (Strength Through Joy) provided free and cheap leisure activities and holidays for workers
- The KdF also helped ordinary Germans buy cheap cars: the Volkswagen (People's Car)

Failure
- Wages and conditions were very poor in the Reich Labour Service
- Trade Unions were banned and all workers had to join the German Labour Front. They lost the right to strike for better pay and conditions
- The diet of working class Germans worsened under the Nazis. Food consumption decreased
- People's average earnings did not change very much

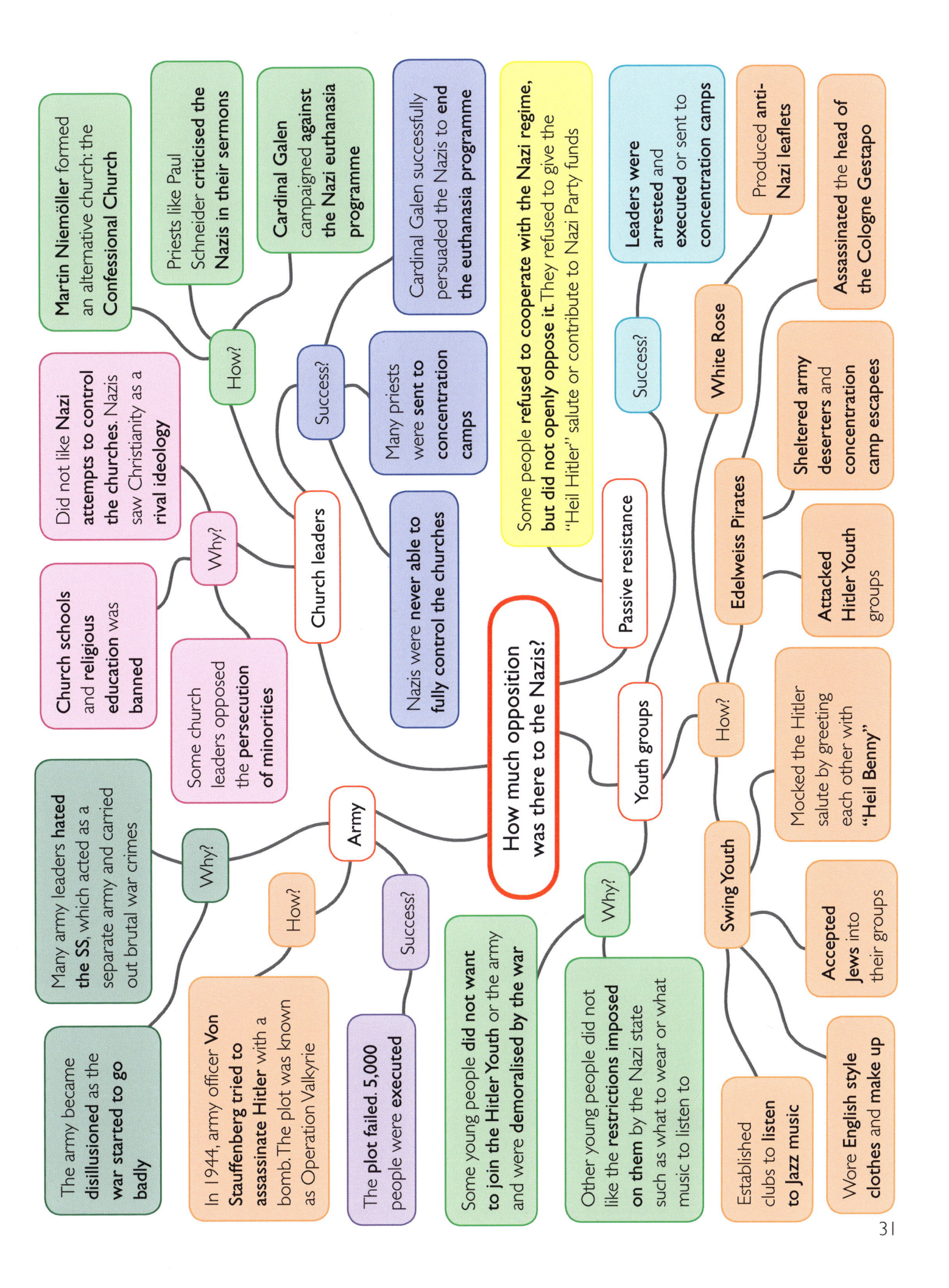

How much opposition was there to the Nazis?

Church leaders

Why?
- Did not like Nazi attempts to control the churches. Nazis saw Christianity as a rival ideology
- Church schools and religious education was banned
- Some church leaders opposed the persecution of minorities

How?
- Martin Niemöller formed an alternative church: the Confessional Church
- Priests like Paul Schneider criticised the Nazis in their sermons
- Cardinal Galen campaigned against the Nazi euthanasia programme

Success?
- Cardinal Galen successfully persuaded the Nazis to end the euthanasia programme
- Many priests were sent to concentration camps
- Nazis were never able to fully control the churches

Army

Why?
- Many army leaders hated the SS, which acted as a separate army and carried out brutal war crimes
- The army became disillusioned as the war started to go badly

How?
- In 1944, army officer Von Stauffenberg tried to assassinate Hitler with a bomb. The plot was known as Operation Valkyrie

Success?
- The plot failed. 5,000 people were executed

Passive resistance

Some people refused to cooperate with the Nazi regime, but did not openly oppose it. They refused to give the "Heil Hitler" salute or contribute to Nazi Party funds

Success?
- Leaders were arrested and executed or sent to concentration camps

Youth groups

Why?
- Some young people did not want to join the Hitler Youth or the army and were demoralised by the war
- Other young people did not like the restrictions imposed on them by the Nazi state such as what to wear or what music to listen to

How?

Swing Youth
- Established clubs to listen to Jazz music
- Wore English style clothes and make up
- Accepted Jews into their groups

Edelweiss Pirates
- Mocked the Hitler salute by greeting each other with "Heil Benny"
- Attacked Hitler Youth groups
- Sheltered army deserters and concentration camp escapees

White Rose
- Produced anti-Nazi leaflets
- Assassinated the head of the Cologne Gestapo

Why did the Nazis persecute certain groups?

Political opponents

- Social Democrats and Communists opposed Nazi ideas and had spoken out against them before 1933
- Many political rivals were killed during the **Night of the Long Knives**

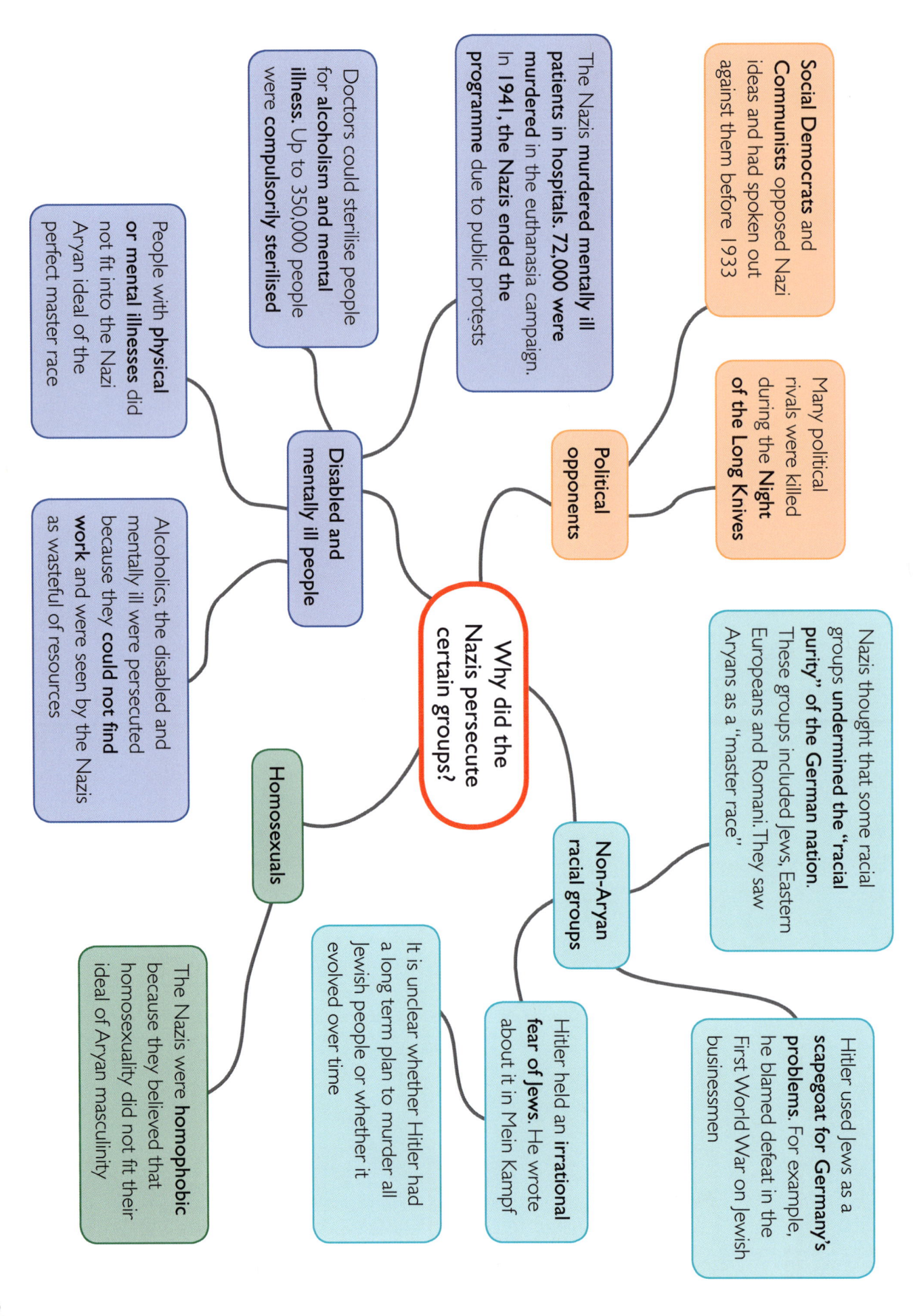

Disabled and mentally ill people

- The Nazis murdered mentally ill patients in hospitals. 72,000 were murdered in the euthanasia campaign. In 1941, the Nazis ended the programme due to public protests
- Doctors could sterilise people for **alcoholism and mental illness**. Up to 350,000 people were **compulsorily sterilised**
- People with **physical or mental illnesses** did not fit into the Nazi Aryan ideal of the perfect master race
- Alcoholics, the disabled and mentally ill were persecuted because they **could not find work** and were seen by the Nazis as wasteful of resources

Non-Aryan racial groups

- Nazis thought that some racial groups undermined the **"racial purity"** of the German nation. These groups included Jews, Eastern Europeans and Romani. They saw Aryans as a "master race"
- Hitler used Jews as a **scapegoat for Germany's problems**. For example, he blamed defeat in the First World War on Jewish businessmen
- Hitler held an irrational **fear of Jews**. He wrote about it in Mein Kampf
- It is unclear whether Hitler had a long term plan to murder all Jewish people or whether it evolved over time

Homosexuals

- The Nazis were **homophobic** because they believed that homosexuality did not fit their ideal of Aryan masculinity

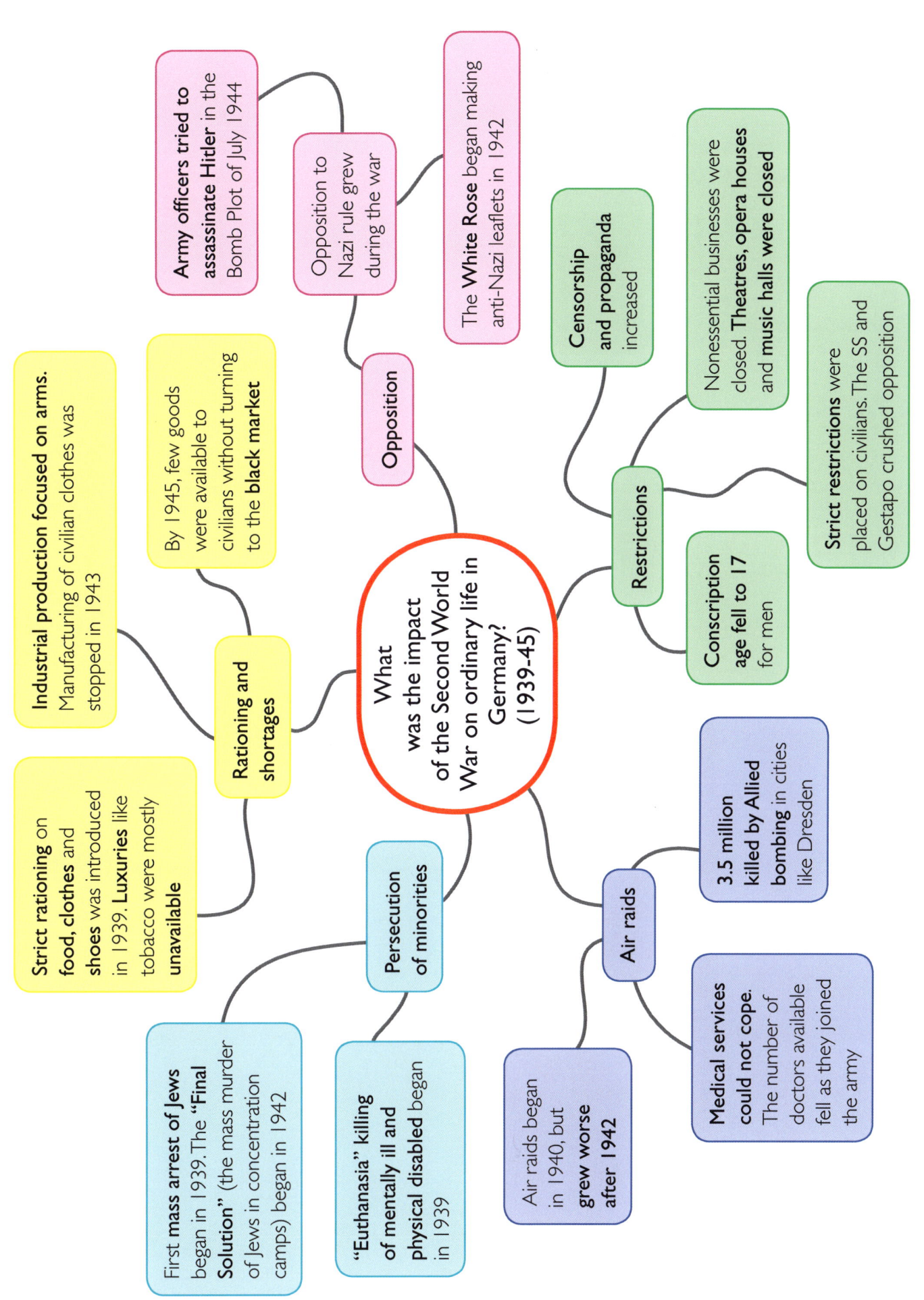

What was the impact of the Second World War on ordinary life in Germany? (1939-45)

Opposition
- Army officers tried to assassinate Hitler in the Bomb Plot of July 1944
- Opposition to Nazi rule grew during the war
- The White Rose began making anti-Nazi leaflets in 1942

Restrictions
- Censorship and propaganda increased
- Nonessential businesses were closed. Theatres, opera houses and music halls were closed
- Strict restrictions were placed on civilians. The SS and Gestapo crushed opposition
- Conscription age fell to 17 for men

Rationing and shortages
- Industrial production focused on arms. Manufacturing of civilian clothes was stopped in 1943
- By 1945, few goods were available to civilians without turning to the black market
- Strict rationing on food, clothes and shoes was introduced in 1939. Luxuries like tobacco were mostly unavailable

Persecution of minorities
- First mass arrest of Jews began in 1939. The "Final Solution" (the mass murder of Jews in concentration camps) began in 1942
- "Euthanasia" killing of mentally ill and physical disabled began in 1939

Air raids
- 3.5 million killed by Allied bombing in cities like Dresden
- Medical services could not cope. The number of doctors available fell as they joined the army
- Air raids began in 1940, but grew worse after 1942

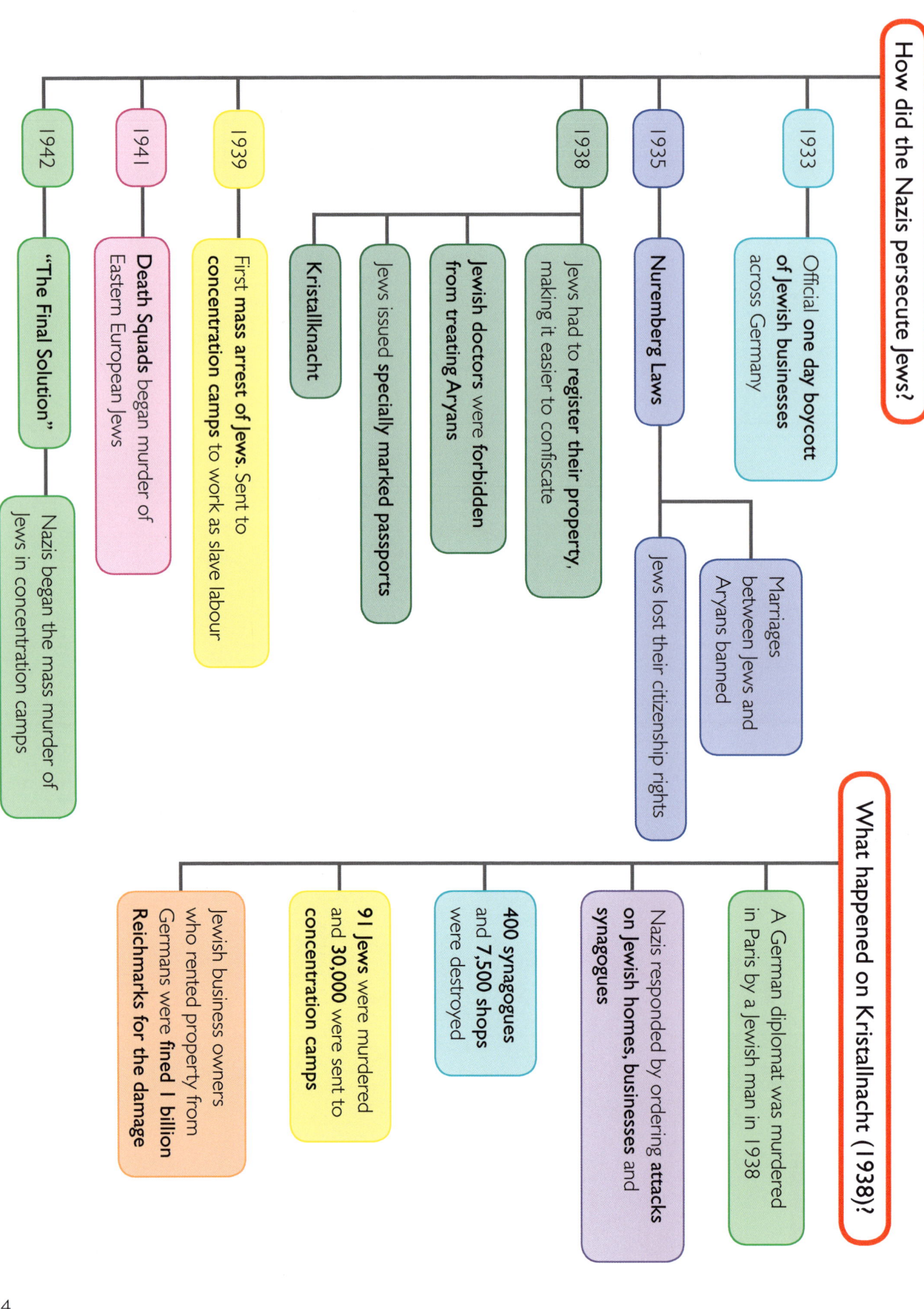

How did the Nazis persecute Jews?

- **1933**: Official **one day boycott of Jewish businesses** across Germany
- **1935**: **Nuremberg Laws**
  - Jews lost their citizenship rights
  - Marriages between Jews and Aryans banned
- **1938**:
  - Jews had to **register their property**, making it easier to confiscate
  - **Jewish doctors** were **forbidden from treating Aryans**
  - Jews issued specially marked passports
  - **Kristallknacht**
- **1939**: First mass arrest of Jews. Sent to **concentration camps** to work as slave labour
- **1941**: **Death Squads** began murder of Eastern European Jews
- **1942**: "**The Final Solution**"
  - Nazis began the mass murder of Jews in concentration camps

What happened on Kristallnacht (1938)?

- A German diplomat was murdered in Paris by a Jewish man in 1938
- Nazis responded by ordering **attacks on Jewish homes, businesses and synagogues**
- **400 synagogues** and **7,500 shops** were destroyed
- **91 Jews** were murdered and **30,000** were sent to **concentration camps**
- Jewish business owners who rented property from Germans were **fined 1 billion Reichmarks** for the damage

34

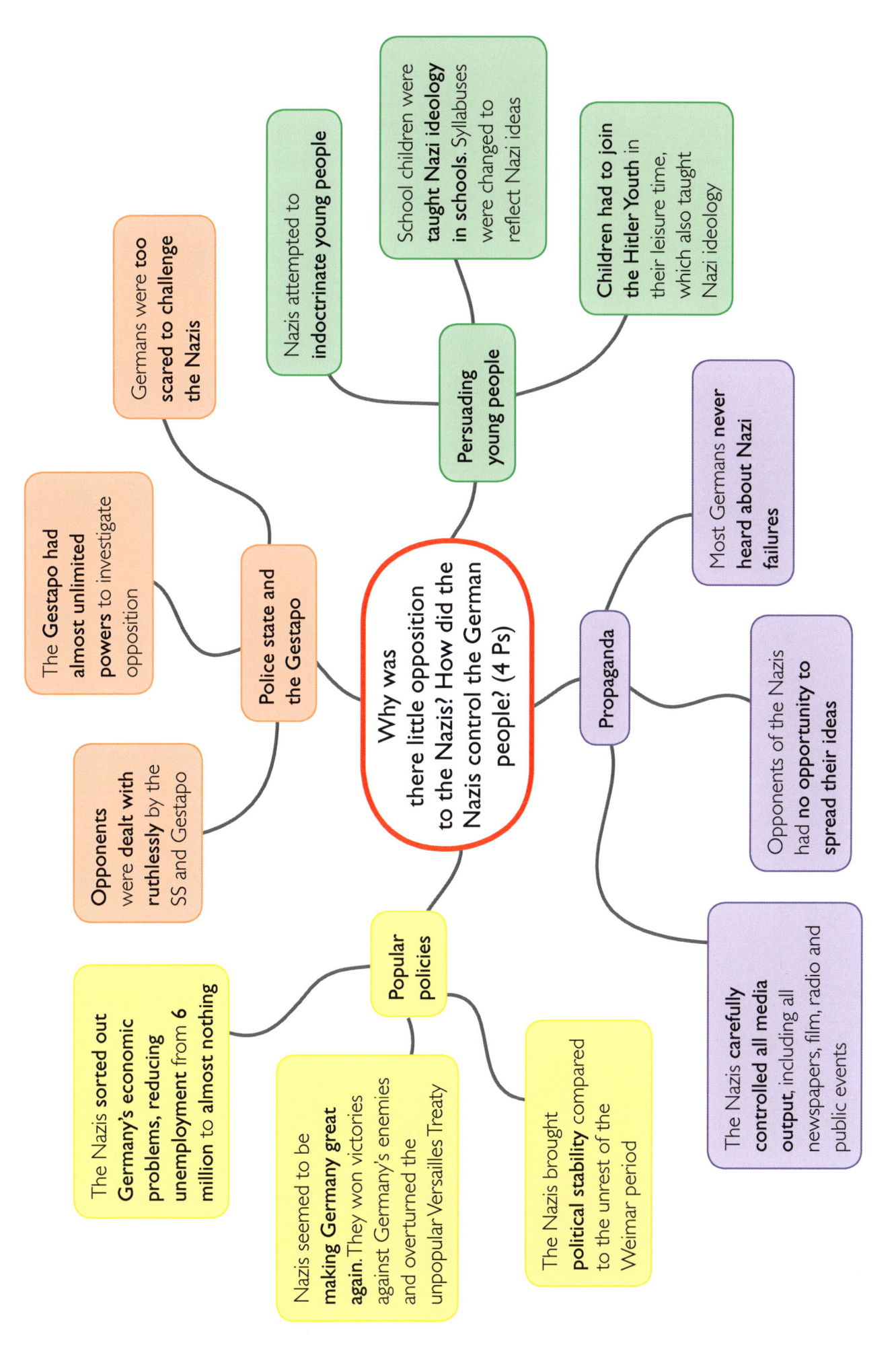

Why was there little opposition to the Nazis? How did the Nazis control the German people? (4 Ps)

Persuading young people
- Nazis attempted to **indoctrinate young people**
- School children were **taught Nazi ideology in schools**. Syllabuses were changed to reflect Nazi ideas
- **Children had to join the Hitler Youth** in their leisure time, which also taught Nazi ideology

Police state and the Gestapo
- Germans were too scared to challenge the Nazis
- The Gestapo had **almost unlimited powers** to investigate opposition
- **Opponents** were **dealt with ruthlessly** by the SS and Gestapo

Propaganda
- Most Germans never heard about Nazi failures
- Opponents of the Nazis had no opportunity to spread their ideas
- The Nazis **carefully controlled all media output**, including all newspapers, film, radio and public events

Popular policies
- The Nazis **sorted out Germany's economic problems**, reducing **unemployment** from 6 million to almost nothing
- Nazis seemed to be **making Germany great again**. They won victories against Germany's enemies and overturned the unpopular Versailles Treaty
- The Nazis brought **political stability** compared to the unrest of the Weimar period

Were German people better off under the Nazis?

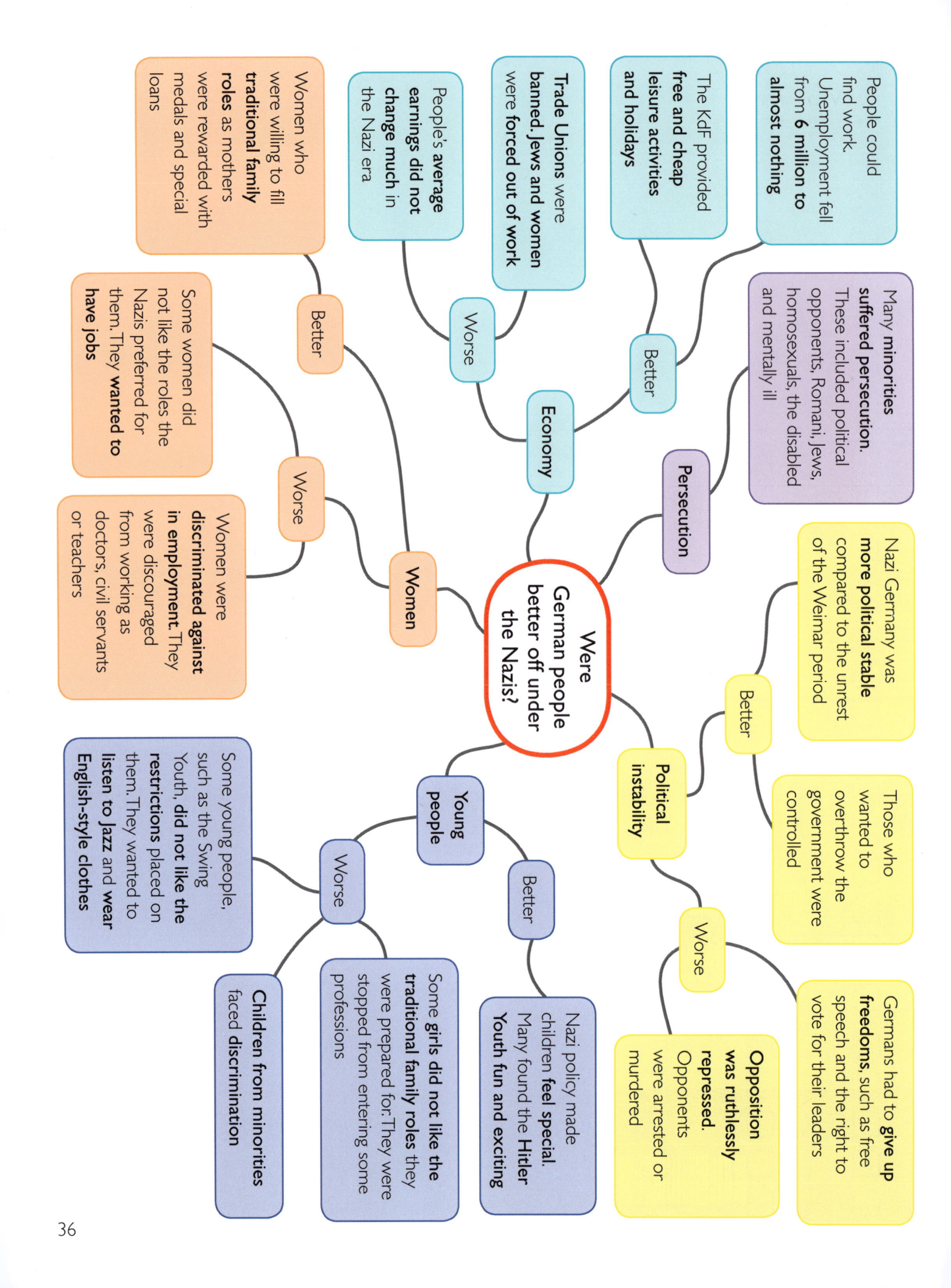

Economy

Better
- People could find work. Unemployment fell from **6 million to almost nothing**
- The KdF provided **free and cheap leisure activities and holidays**

Worse
- **Trade Unions** were banned. Jews and women were **forced out of work**
- People's average earnings did not **change much** in the Nazi era

Persecution
- Many minorities **suffered persecution**. These included political opponents, Romani, Jews, homosexuals, the disabled and mentally ill

Women

Better
- Women who were willing to fill **traditional family roles** as mothers were rewarded with medals and special loans
- Some women did not like the roles the Nazis preferred for them. They **wanted to have jobs**

Worse
- Women were **discriminated against in employment**. They were discouraged from working as doctors, civil servants or teachers

Political instability

Better
- Nazi Germany was **more politically stable** compared to the unrest of the Weimar period
- Those who wanted to overthrow the government were controlled

Worse
- Germans had to **give up freedoms**, such as free speech and the right to vote for their leaders
- **Opposition was ruthlessly repressed.** Opponents were arrested or murdered

Young people

Better
- Nazi policy made children **feel special**. Many found the **Hitler Youth fun and exciting**
- Some girls did not like the **traditional family roles** they were prepared for. They were stopped from entering some professions

Worse
- Some young people, such as the Swing Youth, **did not like the restrictions** placed on them. They wanted to **listen to jazz and wear English-style clothes**
- Children from minorities faced discrimination

36

Revision tracking list

Track your revision by ticking off topics as you learn them.

	Little bit unsure	Fairly confident	Know it!
What happened during the November Revolution (1918)?	☐	☐	☐
What problems did Germany face at the end of the First World War?	☐	☐	☐
What happened during the Spartacist Uprising (1919)?	☐	☐	☐
What happened during the Kapp Putsch (1920)?	☐	☐	☐
What were the strengths and weaknesses of the Weimar Constitution?	☐	☐	☐
What were the terms of the Versailles Treaty?	☐	☐	☐
What was the economic and political impact of the Versailles Treaty (1919)?	☐	☐	☐
What crises did the Weimar Republic face in 1923?	☐	☐	☐
How did Chancellor Stresemann deal with the crises of 1923?	☐	☐	☐
How did the Nazi Party develop before 1923?	☐	☐	☐
What did Hitler and the Nazis stand for in the 1920s?	☐	☐	☐
What happened during the Munich Putsch (1923)?	☐	☐	☐
How did Hitler benefit from the Munich Putsch (1923)?	☐	☐	☐
Why did Hitler think the Munich Putsch would work?	☐	☐	☐
How far did the Weimar Republic recover in the period 1924-29?	☐	☐	☐
How did the Nazis change their tactics in the period 1924-29?	☐	☐	☐
Why were the Nazis not successful in the period 1924-29?	☐	☐	☐
What were the roles of Nazi leaders?	☐	☐	☐
What impact did the Great Depression have on the Weimar Republic?	☐	☐	☐
How did Hitler become Chancellor in 1933?	☐	☐	☐
What was the Reichstag Fire (1933)?	☐	☐	☐
How did the Reichstag Fire benefit Hitler?	☐	☐	☐
Why did Hitler become Chancellor in 1933?	☐	☐	☐
What was the Enabling Act (March 1933)?	☐	☐	☐
How did the Enabling Act benefit Hitler?	☐	☐	☐

	Little bit unsure	Fairly confident	Know it!
How did Hitler become President in 1934?	☐	☐	☐
Why did Hitler make the army swear an oath to him in 1934?	☐	☐	☐
Why were Röhm and the SA seen as a threat by Hitler?	☐	☐	☐
What happened during the Night of the Long Knives (1934)?	☐	☐	☐
Was the Weimar Republic a success or a failure?	☐	☐	☐
How did the Nazis use propaganda?	☐	☐	☐
How successful was Nazi propaganda?	☐	☐	☐
What was the role of the SS and Gestapo? What were concentration camps?	☐	☐	☐
How effective was the Gestapo at controlling the German people?	☐	☐	☐
How did the Nazis control education?	☐	☐	☐
Why did children join the Hitler Youth and the League of German Maidens?	☐	☐	☐
Why did the Nazis want to influence young people?	☐	☐	☐
How successful were Nazi policies towards young people?	☐	☐	☐
What were Nazi policies towards women?	☐	☐	☐
How successful were Nazi policies towards women?	☐	☐	☐
What was wrong with the German economy in 1933?	☐	☐	☐
How did the Nazis reduce unemployment?	☐	☐	☐
How successful were Nazi economic policies?	☐	☐	☐
Did Nazi economic policies make people's lives better?	☐	☐	☐
How much opposition was there to the Nazis?	☐	☐	☐
Why did the Nazis persecute certain groups?	☐	☐	☐
What was the impact of the Second World War (1939-45) on ordinary life in Germany?	☐	☐	☐
How did the Nazis persecute Jews?	☐	☐	☐
What happened on Kristallnacht (1938)?	☐	☐	☐
Why was there little opposition to the Nazis?	☐	☐	☐
How did the Nazis control the German people?	☐	☐	☐
Were German people better off under the Nazis?	☐	☐	☐

Printed in Great Britain
by Amazon